MANIFESTO AOTEAROA

MANIFESTO AOTEAROA

101 POLITICAL POEMS

EDITED BY PHILIP TEMPLE & EMMA NEALE

OTAGO

Published by Otago University Press
Level 1, 398 Cumberland Street
Dunedin, New Zealand
university.press@otago.ac.nz
www.otago.ac.nz/press

First published 2017

ISBN 978-0-947522-46-9

A catalogue record for this book is available from the National Library of New Zealand.

Front cover and internal artwork by Nigel Brown.

Printed in China through Asia Pacific Offset.

CONTENTS

[PART TWO] RIGHTS 61

[PART FOUR] CONFLICT 143

POETRY CHANGES EVERYTHING

Philip Temple

Poetry can begin to change everything when, as Adrienne Rich wrote, it 'lays its hand on our shoulder [and] we are, to an almost physical degree, touched and moved. The imagination's roads open before us, giving the lie to that brute dictum, "There is no alternative".'[1] Nearly 200 years ago, Shelley described poets as the 'unacknowledged legislators of the world', not in the sense of their being lawmakers and bureaucrats but in the sense that poetry is 'the expression of the imagination' of what we are, where we are and what we may yet become, revealing the alternatives to the often oppressive, illogical and even insane dictates of an unimaginative state. Political poems are the most open and cogent expression of democracy, the most vivid and eloquent calls for empathy, for action and revolution, even for a simple calling to account. To paraphrase Franz Kafka, the best political poems should 'be the axe for the frozen sea within us', opening our hearts and minds to what may yet be possible in a chaotic and brutal world.

Political poems have always been part of New Zealand literature. A hundred and thirty years ago, Jessie Mackay parodied Tennyson's 'The Charge of the Light Brigade' in 'The Charge at Parihaka', both poets responding to the absurd actions of deadly power in their time. Eighty years ago, A.R.D. Fairburn published his great social and political sequence *Dominion*, which still speaks to us today with such lines as: '… the land is/ the space between the barbed-wire fences,/ mortgaged in bitterness, measured in sweated butterfat'. Or, for those north of the Bombay Hills, 'This is our paper city, built/ on the rock of debt, held fast/ against all winds by the paperweight of debt'.

In the 1950s, poets like Louis Johnson and James K. Baxter actively challenged the establishment. Johnson wrote:

> It was not our duty to question but to guard,
> maintaining order; see that none escaped
> who may be required for questioning by the State.
> The price was bread and a pension and not a hard
> life on the whole.

Baxter became increasingly evangelical, sharing and reflecting the lives of the outcast and poor:

> But the sweat of work and the sweat of fear
> Are different things to have;
> The first is the sweat of the working man
> And the second of a slave,
> And the sweat of fear turns any place
> Into a living grave.

In the second half of the twentieth century, Māori voices began to be heard in the mainstream world of New Zealand poetry, none more powerfully than Apirana Taylor's:

> My name is Tu the freezing worker
> Ngati D.B. is my tribe
> The pub is my marae
> My fist is my taiaha
> Jail is my home.

There is simply not enough space here to mention or quote all: almost every poet in our history has, at some time, written political poetry. This suggests that perhaps there is another anthology to be assembled of political poems past, because collections of such poetry have been rare. Political poems in New Zealand have tended to be isolated cries, subsumed as part of a greater literary collective. *Manifesto Aotearoa* may prove a useful precedent.

*

I became more aware of the role of writer as critic and conscience of society—especially as the university's part in this was becoming more pusillanimous—when I spent time in Berlin during the late 1980s and 90s. During that period of great change in Germany, the voices of such prominent writers as Günter Grass and Hans Magnus Enzensberger in the west and Christa Wolf in the east were heard and heeded by politicians and media in a way that was unimaginable in New Zealand. Their experience, wisdom and imagination were accepted as part of serious political discourse.

This prompted me at that time, during a period of unsettling change in New Zealand, to use whatever writerly skills I could muster to assist in the changing of our electoral system. Last year, in newly uncertain and threatening times, I was moved to propose this anthology, to bring together voices of protest and imagination that might 'touch and move' and 'give the lie to that brute dictum, "There is no alternative"'. As Bertolt Brecht put it, 'General, man is very useful./ He can fly and he can kill./ But he has one defect:/ He can think.' And: 'Because things are the way they are, things will not stay the way they are.' What they become is up to us, and our poets here show the way.

1 *Guardian*, 18 November 2006.

SONG COMING

Emma Neale

The poet and the politician may both need to be sweet-talkers—artists of verbal persuasion—but they otherwise stand at far corners of the podium. The politician uses words to justify policy; to seduce us to vote; to draw lines between those who deserve and those who don't. The poet often pushes against the boundaries, exploring the grey areas: the ambiguous zones of human emotion and psychology; the subjectivity of experience. The poet's role, too, is often to point out the slippery nature of language itself; to deliberately let multiple meanings play beneath where the light of the word strikes the page.

*

'Poetry makes nothing happen,' said W.H. Auden, in his poem of mourning, 'In Memory of W.B. Yeats'—the kind of aphorism non-poets might use as a counter-argument to the voices of change here. Yet if that is to differentiate it from the language that mobilises troops in proxy wars, bars immigrants, incites violence, allows mining on conservation land, signs devastating trade deals, exits visions of international political unity, or promotes laws that seem predominantly to benefit those already in power—then perhaps 'making nothing happen' is in itself an embodiment of reflective thought: taking time to assess and consider alternative perspectives. The language of poetry is a stage in deeper consideration, reassessment, taking the long view.

Of course Auden's famous poem goes on to counter its own line with: 'it survives/ In the valley of its making where executives/ Would never want to tamper,/ a way of happening, a mouth.' Poetry is not ineffectual; rather it does not force, brutalise, tamper the way those 'executives' (the echo of executioners must be salient) might. It is a way of being that runs counter to the damaging, exploitative corporation; the clinical, interfering functionary; or the flawed institution.

American poet Adrienne Rich has said:

> Art is our human birthright, our most powerful means of access to our own and another's experience and imaginative life. In continually rediscovering and recovering the humanity of human beings, art is crucial to the democratic vision.

Art—poetry—is vital in its ability not only to mirror the present, but to imagine both what we don't have and what we might be. One of its most powerful engines is the human ability to say *if*. Plato famously wanted to banish poets from the ideal republic—on the basis that poets were mere imitators, and could stir up distressing, messy feelings that make happiness and virtue harder to attain. Yet even he actively invites poetry and its defenders to argue their way back in, if they should be able to find that there's a use for poetry other than bringing delight.

What use *is* poetry? As one of our advisory readers, Michael Harlow, often says, imagine a world without poetry, or without song. *Genuinely* envision that, and not only do the 'uses' even of delight itself seem urgently obvious, but many other uses crowd in.

As with all the arts, poetry explains us to ourselves; it explains others to us. It is frequently an act, and a teacher, of empathy. Poetry can give voice to the marginalised. It focuses attention on the overlooked, neglected, the questionably taboo, the too-often unspoken. It shows alternatives to everything from the hollow seductions of consumerism, the reduction of humans to their utility as units of labour, to the dehumanising brutality of violence and porn. It offers therapeutic solace. It can, in fact, seed internal and external change.

In our current political context this anthology is not only a call to protect our environment, a call for equal rights for all, a reminder of the power of the franchise, a plea for non-violence, a reminder of the extremes of suffering experienced by the victims of war and enforced exodus. It is also a reminder of the need for the humanities in general as a corrective to the abuse of power and the starvation of the imagination. If we cannot imagine, there is no hope.

All the poets herein—and the many others who submitted work to us—insist on the healing power of the imagination. They reassure us, as Carolyn McCurdie does in her poem 'Ends', that even at the nadir of despair, if we gather together, we can hear

> song coming.
> Song coming, beyond any
> we've ever before lifted in song.

ABOUT THIS COLLECTION

At the beginning of March 2016 we sent out the call for submissions for *Manifesto Aotearoa*, a collection of new or recent New Zealand political poems. These could 'explore anything from prime ministerial power to the price of milk'. Subjects covered could be 'parliament, the environment, gender issues, political parties, ethnic issues, elections, immigration, religion and power, class, ageism, economics, pressure groups, politicians, the media and much more'. By the deadline of 29 April we had received over 500 poems from more than 200 poets.

Most of the political boxes were ticked and contributors had taken to heart our encouragement that 'poems could be in any form or style', so that the final collection includes work ranging from the lyrical, to erasure poetry, to mock legal documents that skewer questionable policy.

We had also encouraged 'poets of all ethnicities to send us work, including poems in te reo', and we were pleased to receive numerous poems from Māori, Pasifika and Asian contributors. Young and old submitted poems; poets unpublished, slightly published and well published are all represented in the final selection, including five of New Zealand's poets laureate. Our contributors come from across the country, from the Bay of Islands to Bluff.

With space to include only about 20 per cent of the poems submitted, we were faced with a demanding and tortuous process of selection. We moved from one long list to another until we arrived at the final 101, applying an essential dictum of only one poem per poet. (The three exceptions prove the rule.) Some poems, no matter how good, were put to one side because we felt they did not have sufficient political focus or edge. Some poems, again no matter how good, were set aside because they repeated the theme of another we liked a little more, or which fitted a sequence better. We could easily have included more if space had allowed.

As we read through the poems, four broad categories emerged that have subsequently made up the sections of this book.

The generally political section, 'Then what do people here die of?' includes poems about politicians and parliament, capitalist society, the international political experience and surveillance.

The rights section, 'A stone in the mouth of the people', includes poems of protest and often outrage about the plight of working people and the poor, gender inequalities of power, the place and rights of Māori and challenges to the governing social system.

The environment section, 'Taking selfies by the ruins', includes poetry of lament about the destruction and poisoning of our landscapes and our alienation from the natural environment.

The conflict section, 'Behind every human shield is another human shield', includes poems that move from images of war and violence to powerfully reflect a world of refugees and displacement. They appeal for disarmament, speak of oppression and violence at home, and express deep unease about our future.

We are glad we undertook the task of putting together this striking collection which, in many ways, reflects who and where New Zealanders are today. Thank you to all who submitted poems and especial thanks to those who actively aided and encouraged us: our contributing editors Hinemoana Baker, Diane Brown, Michael Harlow, Vincent O'Sullivan and Brian Turner; and Rachel Scott, Imogen Coxhead and Fiona Moffat of Otago University Press. We are all indebted to artist Nigel Brown for, pro bono, providing us with such a grand cover painting and the striking images throughout the book.

Philip Temple and Emma Neale

FROM
MISTER SPEAKER
TIGHTEN HANDCUFFS ON PROTESTORS WRISTS
NOT OUT OF THE WOODS YET
I'LL GIVE YOU LACK
BIG TOURIST PICTURES
HAPPY VOTERS
NEW FLAG SILVER AND BLUE
MY POLLS TELL ME THE PEOPLE LOVE ME
SECTIONS 52 S
3
DELIVER US FROM SCARCE RESOURCES
POLITICS
WHAT DO PEOPLE DIE
THE
GRABBERS ARE EVERYWHERE
CAUTERISED NATURE
DISINCENTIVIZE
THE ENDLESS
FINANCIAL YEAR
PRIVATISE THE NIGHT
BULK BELLIGERENCE BATTERY
IN A BLINK IF THEY COULD
SMOOCHY DEALS
THE HIRE PATH
WHEN
DOORS ARE LEFT AJAR
RED IS THE MOST FUGITIVE COLOUR
ALYOSHA - SHA SHKUMBINI RIVER
LIKE THE COMPANY OF FOOLS
WE WERE

[PART ONE] POLITICS

Then what do people here die of?

—Vincent O'Sullivan

The (Andrew) Little things

David Eggleton

By the right quick march.
There was the I AM that am, the right abominable Arrrr
Muldoon, but we saw him off—
Mister Speaker, Mister Speaker.

Then the invasion of the Rogergnomes,
after-hours on the phones,
selling off the family silver—
Mister Speaker, Mister Speaker.

Bolger gave the district the old once-over,
from the driving seat of his Land-Rover:
get off the grass, ya greenie greenhorn,
or I'll make you wish you'd never been born—
Mister Speaker, Mister Speaker.

And the Ruthenasia razor-gang brought trouble:
tramp, tramp, trample of coppers on the double;
the smooth slick slide of the right sort of card,
as the greasy ball went flying from the ruck ruck ruck—
Mister Speaker, Mister Speaker.

Next, we scuttled the unsinkable Ssss Shipley
as Enzed moved from riot riot riot to totally dead quiet,
around the turn of the century,
following Hanoi Helen's gumboot diplomacy—
Mister Speaker, Mister Speaker.

Now there's the d'oh, ray, meh
of craptacular Don Key,
and the twerky-jerky tweet-tweets of the shiny whiny Gnats
riffing along to banksta raps—
Mister Speaker, Mister Speaker.

Crusher Collins is no longer crushed, and I get no thrill
from Jumbotron Bill and his double-breasted pin-stripe crew,
who read their script from prophetic scrolls of fern:
steady as it goes, till it's gone—
Mister Speaker, Mister Speaker.

Watch that backstairs operator, the arch manipulator,
Eminem McCully carried shoulder high:
it's an endless blue of lies,
of ginger-snap altercations, Jesus sunbeams,
fruitcakes and custard pies—
Mister Speaker, Mister Speaker.

The ACT member for the good people of Epsom
has assumed the missionary position for corporate consultation,
as land sharks preach to cash cow convertors;
and they are drug-testing the tree-loggers,
but what about the bloggers—
Mister Speaker, Mister Speaker.

Noisy as a giant baby's rattle, all the social media prattle:
tittle-tattle about Kim Dot-who? disguised as a giant weta
feeding on slaters in a petting zoo in Remuera,
to the sound of wobbly possum laughter—
Mister Speaker, Mister Speaker.

So they're digging up the foundations
for better fibre-optic relations
with new techno empires needing lackey nations
who will fetch and carry,
and look in every nook and cranny for a buck—
Mister Speaker, Mister Speaker.

And will they tighten handcuffs on protesters' wrists,
so they cannot shake their fists—

Objection, objection—

Objection sustained! Sustained! Sustained!

First reading

Alex Taylor

I.

it is a bow tie with a business jacket
it is a bad wave job with a cream cravat
it is a blank stare and looking at his nails
it is check with stripes and *reading off the same song sheet*
it is fondling the other microphone

it is a mauve tie and red sashes with a regal nose
it is a thick flat new zild accent with a bald spot
it is a shade of purple for a beauty pageant
it is the cheshire cat on a soapbox

it is the old guard or the new deal
it is *what i will say* and *let's deal in facts*
it is *arrant nonsense* and a yellow highlighter

II.

everyone is standing up
the big gold stick comes in the
clerks are hunch-shouldered and
his cheeky wave down the aisle

it is *internal emassinations*, which doesn't sound quite right
it is a salt or pepper suit with evangelising hands

i seek to leave. the source of the document.
the slipped tongue, does it come fully furnished?
eric is upside down on colorado

it is a fruit bowl on a blouse
it is *unable to fill a telephone booth* if he tried

the wide eyes and the brow
hands like a trampoline and *running*
up and down the country; a bio man
hits a purple patch with a patsy

it is the voice loudest to the wall
it is charisma on a budget

he is a big man to take issue
with a red sequin tie *we're not out*
of the woods yet whose head like an
upside-down egg never looks up

it is hair across her face and *floundering on benefits*
it is *the true nature of the left* and the same bowtie as the day before

she is trying to match her hair
to a salmon cardie the person
behind has a half pint of water
it looks like anyway *zip it*
sweetie i'm getting there and the
solution is simple we can continue
to grow on that *an investment*
approach and *a bouncy economy*

it is a wagging finger with a widow's peak
it is lost revenue and spectacular eyebrows
it is difficult to tell if it is a prediction or a production

Power riddle

Cilla McQueen

Running free
or harboured in cells
not your cells
and not by bees
nor kept by keys
I sting quick as malice

I split trees
rock holds me to its heart
it queers the compass
I can make the sky explode
Interrupt me? Hah!
I'll give you lack.

To miss the point entirely

Vincent O'Sullivan

It isn't good for a writer to live in a country
where a cut-price banker with his next-door smile
is all we have to throw stones at. How one
envies a Chilean say who could dream of knifing
a home-grown monster, the English even
who might smash a TV any day of the year
when a government of schoolboys simper as if Matron
threatened to punish arse.
'A country without snakes!'
as tourists at times are amazed to hear. 'Then what
do people here die of?', another traveller once
asked me. 'Of being ourselves,' I told him,
'the big tourist pictures falling off the wall with mould.'

A song for happy voters

Kevin Ireland

Happy days are here again,
we've the leaders we deserve,
there's Tricky Dick and Tommy Rot
and Snappy Sam the Swerve.

Double their pay and give them all
the grubby power they need
for Dick's corrupt but awfully nice
and Tom's an ace for greed

and dear old Sid's the best there is
and when the widows cry
he sheds a tear himself and swears
he wouldn't harm a fly.

Those who voted for these scamps
have earned their blessed sleep.
Our butcher-boys look after us
as wolves watch over sheep.

The General wants a new flag

Frankie McMillan

The General thinks he has it all stitched up. Soon his new flag will fly over both islands. He stares at himself in the mirror. His chin has been slightly nicked while shaving. He turns to present his good side, the heavy medals clanking on his chest. 'At the end of the day …' he begins. He tries again, this time from his speech notes. The words Battle of Chunuk Bair and Battle of the River Plate have been underlined in red. 'Too much bloody red,' he murmurs. The colour makes him uneasy. His new flag will be silver and blue. His new flag will fly triumphant over land and sea. Already the wave of support crashes around his shores, already the rumble of stones courses through the streets. One of the stones strikes the window. He peers out. Down below is a great crowd. Rabble rousers! Some of them are in wheelchairs. Some are old soldiers, some look hungry. 'What do we want?' a loudspeaker blares. 'Food!' the people chant. The General tightens his jacket. He leans over the parapet. 'My people,' he cries. 'Can't a man chew and walk at the same time?' The crowd hurl their worn shoes at him. The General retreats. He is the General of not one island but two, yet at this very moment, glancing at himself in the mirror, he sees only his nicked chin, the slight trickle of blood.

My people

Philip Temple

My people tell me
those cries in the distance
are cheers waffled
by the wind

My polls tell me
the people love me
fronting the lens under
the lights on the podium

My people tell me
those banners below
cannot be read
in the dark

My polls tell me
they do not count
the ones who quote me
rights in their odium

I tell my people
spin the wheel
spin the deal
let them enjoy
their own conclusions

Serving notice upon the prime minister

Siobhan Harvey

An amendment to 1986 Residential Tenancies Act
Relating to a state house (definition: *a house owned by the state*) **located at 260 Tinakori Road, Wellington**

Section 51 Termination by notice

(1) Subject to **Sections 52, 53, 53A, 59** and **59A**, the minimum period of notice required to be given by the majority to terminate the tenancy of 260 Tinakori Road, Wellington, shall be as follows:

(a) where we, the majority, owners of all state houses require all state houses as the principal place of residence for us, the majority, or any members of our whanau, 42 days;
(b) where we, the majority, use state houses, or have acquired state houses, for occupation by our neighbours, that fact being clearly stated in the tenancy agreement of 260 Tinakori Road, Wellington, 42 days;
(c) where we, the majority give vacant possession of 260 Tinakori Road, Wellington, to a new tenant, 42 days.

(2) Subject to **Sections 52, 53, 53A, 59** and **59A**, where we, the majority, have given an effective notice to terminate the tenancy of 260 Tinakori Road, Wellington, we, the majority, may at any time before the expiry of the notice enforce immediate termination of that tenancy where actions undertaken by the Prime Minister, or that party's agents, are shown to have misled or affected unjustly the interests of the majority.

(3) Subject to **Sections 52, 53, 53A, 59** and **59A**, where we, the majority, have given an effective notice to terminate the tenancy of 260 Tinakori Road, Wellington, the Prime Minister, or that party's agents, are obliged to notice that they are on notice.

(4) Subject to **Sections 52**, **53**, **53A**, **59** and **59A**, every notice to terminate the tenancy of 260 Tinakori Road, Wellington shall:

(a) be in writing, in voice, in debate, in marching, in banner waving, in hikoi, in referenda, in voting and/or in blood; and
(b) identify the Prime Minister and that party's agents to which it relates; and
(c) specify the date by which the Prime Minister and that party's agents are to vacate 260 Tinakori Road, Wellington; and be signed in writing, in voice, in debate, in marching, in banner waving, in hikoi, in referenda, in voting and/or in blood by us, the majority.

The head of department's prayer on a change of government

Keith Westwater

Our Minister, who art in Cabinet,
hallowed be thy name.
Thy party won,
thy will be done,
in fact as it is in fiction.
Give us this day your empty signifiers,
And cover our stuff-ups,
as we cover yours when you pot us.
And lead us not into the glare of scrutiny,
but deliver us from scarce resources.
For thine is the government,
the power and the spin,
at least until the next election.

Amen/Awomen

Bite the bright coin its brilliance

Michael Harlow

The 'Grabbers', they are everywhere
such a dark swarm; and they clone
themselves, that's more than a worry.
Instinct with egomania, that's more
than a name ...

1. They say you may be truly gifted, the good fortune that
you yourself have made. Your hands are everywhere that
swells the purse. You say there is a decency that winner
takes all, and all there is to be taken. Trust your reach for the
'good as gold'. Bite the bright coin its brilliance

2. Take hold, then and pleasure yourself. And a delighting kiss in the
mirror as silky as the moon's touch. Keep spies to tell you everything.
Have ears everywhere

3. Blazoning of headlines be starbright to dazzle the public
eye. Be the emperor of the Midas horde

4. Here's how to pilfer and filch and be happy too. Stash the
all of it in your best bank. Then put the bank in a box.
Carefully, put the box in the dark of your pocket. On the
way out a bravura flourish turn all the locks to silly to such
helplessness as will confound the world. And slip away as
stealthily as you entered the richness of your time

5. Homeward bound then, a pleasure that in you swells. To
the cars in their stalls buffed to a sheen. To the dear wife
who is reading a book about how and how often. Already
she is stripping down to her birthday. You might think that
heaven is no further away than a 'quick one'. To the kids
who have been caressed to sleep by nanny. Who is quite a
number herself

6. And now as you open the door, slip through, a shine in your eye with flowers for more of the same. With a fat sigh that has your name all over it—call it a day richly spent. And a life too.

Boom

Richard Reeve

They arrive in new-model cars, wear Hilfiger, are gracious.
One swears she gave birth to you; another you need a hand.
They rate dogs over cats. Vote Jurassic over Cretaceous,

believe in comfortable distraction, times of getting rich
doing nothing more remarkable than visiting children.
They show a willingness to travel, a talent for kitsch.

On the topic of culture, they refer to the Festival,
trans-Atlantic gurus, the impossible grinning conductor;
the hip hop acapella from Soweto they liked best of all,

but liked too the Pasifika poet who discussed on air
her reef-bright childhood, liked a troupe of marionette dancers,
liked the irrebuttable author with her scrawl of hair.

Like driving to Beethoven among the shadows of mountains.
Theirs is the royal jelly of experience, keeps flowing;
pensively they idle in the gardens with their fountains.

While the others, the also-rans, subverted to their opinions,
mutter minor misgivings at the unremitting kindness
that has cauterised nature, turned poets into minions.

Procyclical

Nick Ascroft

The fire sales of the night sky chart untold hellish hotspots,
where the laws of supply and demand, investment insecurity

and spit-in-the-handshake goodwill policy hold in cross-cutting,
top-down orbits. And every star-orb reveals another innumerable

thousand hells at the depreciating edges of its occultation.
The galaxies are peppered with estate agents' inflated

quotations. There's a mortgage in every arc-second of the heavens
deadlocked on a dead-end job. But the ejecta of every sector

bleed opportunity; every crash event has its equal and opposite.
Before the nova is a supergiant bubble, over-extending

on itself. It's procyclical. No implosion or downturn need
disincentivise the optimism of nimble mass. At the cutting

edge of the known universe, new markets are radiating back
with enterprise, money-money-money, professional indifference

and the endless financial year.

How they came to privatise the night

Maria McMillan

It began with shadows
Our dark selves
Small nights we carry with us
Stretched and shrunk
Rushed into corners

Striding into the sky
Like the Chinese lovers
Whose bridge is the Milky Way—
Distance was nothing to them
Or waiting seven years.

Clearly of private benefit
They said: The shade they offer.
The company. The sense of self.
Hitherto pricing has not reflected
Their true value.

~

Dusk was much the same.
A wilful resistance
To applying the forces
Of the market.
The stillness.

The nuances of colour.
The way mountains seem closer
And the white houses
On the hills of the city
Shine like angels.

~

Then night.
By the time we heard
The sun had slipped between
the South Island and the sea.
Gone like music at a party
You are walking away from.
Night was a business.

The government maintains
A regulatory role.
At the end of every street
Yellow-jacketed officers collect tariffs.
They watch for you.

Watering the garden
In the coolness.
Talking in quiet voices
On the porch;
Inside the kids dream.

Letting the cat in and out.
Opening the curtain to sneak
A glimpse of the orange
Mouth of moon.

Functions are contracted out—
Absence of light.
Comfort to the weary.
Frost. Fear. Astronomy.
Navigation. Romance.

The dark profusions of freesias
Letting go of themselves.

Rugby

Brian Turner

A sport not a pastime, where bulk,
                    belligerence and battery
go hand in hand with courage,
                    athleticism and skill,

and the bounce of the ball's
                    unreliable—insouciant
one could say—as well as fickle,
                    and where indecision

joins, packs down with chance
                    and relentless coldblooded
calculation; and balance and thinking
                    quickly while on one's feet are
indispensible, to be treasured.

But who would play it today
                    if fortune didn't come with fame?

Tornado funnel

Vivienne Plumb

Instant cash loans fifty metres
states the sign attached to an empty
clapped-out truck parked by the road.
The wind rises and the dust and grit
whips itself up
into a scary mini-tornado on Tuam,
just around C4.

Duke Street is blocked by a crane
as big as Nicky Minaj's arse.
Please Report to the Construction Office
in wobbly pink dazzle-paint.

Late in the afternoon,
there's only one lone car
parked down the back,
cramped with suss-looking
hi-vis dudes. *Who dey*?

Smoochy deals and rorts are going down
in every wide-boy wasteland corner,
kissy-kiss future constructions
are agreed over a cowboy shake and a wink.
A human of no visible gender,
attired in a Total Asbestos Removal
onesie with matching booties,
mask, hood and gloves,
scrip-scrapes away at a ridge of whatever
on a gutted crusty city lot.

A thunder-black Pajero is crouched
outside its matching four-bedroom home
for sale on Fendalton: *owners moving to Perth*
and require a quick sale on this wonderful home.

Excuses, excuses, someone's leaving town,
lugging a suitcase of hopes and dreams
that only departure can fulfil.
The other jealous residents whisper, and confess,
they'd go in a blink, if only they could.

Enlightenment

Beverly Martens

To those seeking
enlightenment
Eastern mystics suggest
chopping wood
and carrying water

And then
from the moment
of Nirvana
much the same.

Here the powers-that-be
point out higher education
as the way forward

Get the marks they say
to make your way
before logging on
three years later
to SEEK—the hire path

Only now
carrying debt
and sipping
bottled water.

watchtower

Luke Sole

she knocks loudly three times
the good word doesn't have time for trousers
so i open the door in a neil young t-shirt and underpants
and listen as she juggles her watchtowers
and hands me the one with a big tank in flames
explaining that syria and trump are all part of it
and her mother always said that problems start
when doors are left ajar
so perhaps a big wall isn't such a bad idea
and i nod and ask if i can keep the one
with castro in fatigues and more flames
and she tells me they are busy letting god in
and maybe he'll arrive next year

A display case in the Museum of Communism

David Howard

1

What if there are fistfights in the bread lines?
Poetry's half a meal. Don't go hungry.

While people sleep off alcohol on their feet,
dream of dancing pumps, a young ballerina's smile.

They used to stay up all night to count tanks
today they stare at your red shirt.

However bold, red is the most fugitive colour.

2

Extract resin from pine trees for turpentine
turning a starling from a swallow's nest.

When it was early birds
circled homeward, from here

we hear a drummer boy.

3

Andrei Stepanovich Arzhilovsky
a boy catches carp with silver scales and a bird's tail.

We are in a world observed by Chagall
and the secret police. If somebody hiccups

it is a denunciation in triplicate. Rat-a-tat-tat!
Tell me about the invisible

Andrei Stepanovich, all the usual hassles
queuing for bread or the grave, saluting

birds of prey: they celebrate Vissarionovich
he rolls the executions on his tongue like berries.

Tell me about the invisible
their gestures are ironic, such a simple thing

the human mechanism:
with this happy life of ours what is there left

not to hurt? Socialism is soup made of cow lips.
Smack smack.

Papa has taken his place with God
Liza is pressing butter at the Collective, Galina

splits stolen timber for both stoves, they took
down Nikisha's barn, they're picking up

the wheat under the floorboards
kernel by kernel.

The starlings disappear, then the stars
yet soldiers march faster in darkness

and sing: 'Alyosha, sha!—take a half-tone lower, stop
telling lies.' The factory's whistle sounds hoarse.

Those shadows are the ghosts of the first Politburo
Trotsky Zinoviev Kamenev Sokolnikov Bubnov

and a small boy with a toy drum, rat-a-tat-tat!

4

The sun doesn't rise for one side of the street
it shines on one side of the street.

When there are strands of long hair
expect an investigation. When there are none

expect an investigation to produce twenty.
Enter that crematorium, the State

where your mother and father must live
with Uncle K. in a filing cabinet.

By the gates two trees stand at attention.
Their leaves have no shadows.

The shadows have been taken for questioning.
Collect the dirt from under

Uncle K.'s fingernails, the dirt
behind Grandmother's eyelids, the dirt

between the toes of the Madonna.

5

In the yard two strangers on opposite sides of a well
looking into the darkness, silent.

After mystery, peace; stunned enemies become friends
because we need one another

to haul up the bucket, to empty our memories into it
each one longer than the tail of a meteorite

then to send the bucket through the night, again.

6

We were assigned a field
to dream, sleeping with one another under stars

their light sharpened the sickles beside us
so, being free to choose, we could

cut the flowers for our funeral.

Voluntary labour on the Shkumbini River, Albania

September 1973

Chris Else

The shift we were working on
stopped for a break as the sun

dipped below the Western edge
of the valley. The cool shade

rolled over us. We sat and ate
salami and black bread, watched

as the rising tide of dusk crept
up the Eastern slope. The seep

of evening took over half an hour before
the terraced fields, the olive groves, the mountain pasture

darkened, leaving a bright, high thread
of silver where the last rays touched the ridge.

All around me there was soft-toned
talk I did not understand

and someone laughed with the carefree
grace of a young mind. Way up there,

where the now dark wedge of earth met
the cobalt sky I saw a light,

a tiny speck of gold. I asked Muhamet
what it was. 'A house,' he said.

‘Somebody lives there. When they electrified
the country, the Party decided

no one would miss out.’
It was a proud boast.

I wondered at such simple faith
and then the lights went on around the work site

and the ground on which we sat exploded
into a jagged mass of rock and shadow.

We got to our feet and picked up our tools
and, like the company of fools

we were, we began to sing.

From *The Little Ache: A German notebook*

Ian Wedde

28

Kropotkin Vodka
was the title of the Pussy Riot song that came to mind
by the overflowing rubbish bins and empty bottles
near the Russian War Memorial in Treptower Park
where I hoped some twenty-first-century Proudhonists
might have been partying overnight
in honour of Peter Kropotkin
whose unbending anarchist principles
were a few clicks to the left
of Sozialdemokrat Johannes Wedde.

I like to imagine
that my distant relative's presence as a German delegate
at the First Congress of the Second International
in Paris in 1889
was noted by Kropotkin
on account of the exclusion of anarcho-syndicalists from the congress,
a remit supported by the 'German Marxists'.

Little did Kropotkin know
while sucking angry spit from his beard
in Bromley High Street,
Greater London,
that his place of exile would one day
add Siouxsie Sioux and Poly Styrene to its alumni
thus stitching together another of those
'webs of significance'
since both punk singers are cited as role models
by Pussy Riot.

The grim parterre of the war memorial
the aggrandising monumentality of its architecture

the bad faith of its lugubrious statues
and fatuous bas-relief narratives
were deserving of an anarchic Pussy Riot party
but I had to make do with the underground moles
whose modest subversions
had built memorial-mounds across the picnic grounds
of Treptower Park.

Little homages to peaceful coexistence
to which I later raised a glass of icy Stoli
during the din of Happy Hour
at the Kino bar on the corner.

A revolutionary sonnet

Koenraad Kuiper

The prescription is that:
the coffee should be good,
in a brown café for the intellectuals.

Since the tea ladies have received their
notices marked private and confidential in red,
they are being asked for their reaction.

So it goes with the firing squad.
It is rightly the intellectuals who are lined up first.
They are in the way of the revolution because
they drink good coffee served in brown cafés.

I have talked to Stalin about this.
I have talked to Mao.
In Europe they still have some intellectuals
and the revolution never comes.

Streets of Kiev

Stephen Oliver

after Osip Mandelstam

In Red Square, giant plasma screens loom blank
and wall-eyed, there's no news today. The Kremlin

thug needs time to think. He never counts his
losses, pays no heed to them. His mongoloid eyes

turn unperturbedly to the southwest. Any day now,
he will perform the prisyadka* in Khreshchatyk Street.

Under the black belt moon, he cocks one leg,
a kick to the solar plexus, to the groin, to the temple.

Pectorals flex, abs ripple. His favourite cocktail,
Polonium-210, he serves up to those who dare oppose.

His expression resembles that of a firing squad,
this former KGB analyst calculates the odds quiet

as frost at midnight, his every move accounted for:
pieces of tibia, femur, cranium, each precious object

finds a place on his chessboard. Any day now,
he will perform the prisyadka in Andreevsky Spusk.

---

* *Prisyadka*: the squat-and-kick move that belongs to the Ukrainian 'Cossack Dance' known as Kazatsky.

First impressions

Paula Green

Vice-President Spiro Agnew brought his wife,
an Apollo 10 astronaut, a fleet of newsmen
and a score of aides to spread his message of goodwill
through the Pacific,
but hundreds of long-haired ruffians stood outside
the Intercontinental Hotel in Auckland
yelling, 'One two three four
we don't want your stupid war.'

He could tell in a flash they were
the brown-rice, I-Ching ruffians
the kidney-bean, carrot-cake-with-cream-cheese ruffians
the Carlos-Castaneda, LSD ruffians
the Ban-the-Bomb, Give-Peace-a-Chance ruffians
the Mother-Earth, home-birth ruffians
the Be-Here-Now, flower-power ruffians
the I-love-Woodstock, Moosewood-cookbook ruffians
(give a year or two).

He could tell that in an instant.

After all the kerfuffle and the police batons drawn,
he raised his eyebrows, shrugged his shoulders
and said with all the goodwill in the world,
'They have nothing constructive to offer.'

New Year cartoons

C.K. Stead

21.1.13

Prince Harry compares
killing Afghans from
an Apache gunship
to computer games—

PlayStation for example.
With practised thumbs
and a small royal brain
he does it well.

His dad's delighted—
says he's 'Making
the Nasties keep
their heads down.'

28.1.13

After Obama's
second victory
the Republican Party
is unhappy.

He will take away
the guns America needs
to defend itself
against itself.

In Virginia
they want to change
the rules so Romney
would have won.

29.1.13

Speaking to reporters
on Holocaust
Memorial Day
Signor Berlusconi

who has been reading
Mussolini's letters
has a kind word
for Il Duce.

It's true he sent
Jews to Wherever-it-was
but his help to Hitler was
'not entirely conscious'.

1.2.13

Iran has sent
a monkey into space
and brought it back
(this time) alive.

Iran has oil,
Iran has heavy water.
Now Iran has a simian
astronaut-survivor.

And on Iran TV—look
here's a new device
for sawing off
the hands of thieves.

6.2.13

America's new
Secretary of State
John Kerry
first day in the job

sends a message
congratulating us
on the anniversary
of our Waitangi Treaty.

He thinks we've set
the world an example.
So has he—start
with the easy stuff.

8.2.13

In Leicester
a dig has discovered
a king in a carpark—
his broken skull

and crook-back spine
confirming this is
Shakespeare's
story-book killer

of the boys in the Tower
who lost a kingdom
only for want of
'*A horse, a horse!*'

10.2.13

As much as
twenty-nine per cent
of your United Kingdom
beefburger

may have pulled
a Romanian cart
or run a race
or chased a fox

but don’t complain—
it’s good protein and free
of detectable feline
or canine traces.

12.2.13

Why am I shocked
his Holiness has
chucked it in?
Shouldn’t he have died

like the old Pole
in agonies
of age and office?
What’s the job

for God’s sake?
‘*Pain*,’ I hector,
‘*Pain!* Isn’t that the
name of the Game?’

20.2.13

On ‘Kill-list Tuesdays’
the President
signs off the names
of those who are to die

far from Washington,
usually at home.
Ever efficient
the United States

doesn’t need to put
a Prince up there
thumb on the button.
They do it by drone.

An international poetry festival in Vietnam

Sue Wootton

The authorities are nervous. It's risky
to bring in the poets. When they say *flower*
are they speaking of flowers?

It's risky for the poets. It can lame a poet,
bearing these poems. They are avid, intent. Absorbed,
absorbing, and their poems fatten, loom.

When they recite they offer words like flowers
if the flowers were strewn like limbs
and the limbs reclaimed

and the bones ground
in a mortar with the spit of the ancestors
ground and ground with a heavy granite pestle

so as to dissolve under the tongue
of the enemy, so as to restart the heart.

The Greater Wall

Liang Yujing

You really don't have to go to North China
To worship its magnificence, the Great Wall
Whose megaliths are timeworn and loose
Unable to keep away any foe

We've built a new one, a magic construction
And named it the Greater Wall
This one, thinner than scrim, lighter than air
Encloses a yard of 9600 square kilometres
Much larger than before

The Greater Wall is everywhere, its acidic shadow
Eating into our marble faces, burning our breath
Our eyeballs turning up and down
In the rockbound eyepits
Struggling to see more
But nothing else, only the—

Wall that spreads like SARS
Wall that creeps like cats
Wall that flows like thoughts
Wall that falls like bombs
We, frog-like, leap this way and that
Getting dried, our flattened skins hung out
On the smooth and blank surface
Of the—

Wall that rolls on wheels
Wall that extends along streets
Wall that lingers in publishing houses
Wall that rushes down from Himalayas
Diving into the Yangtze, floats all the way

To Cathayan valleys and plains
And freezes the East China Sea

Where we're halfway drowning, eyes wildly open
Amazed by the omnipresence of the
Wall in schools in stores in parks in cinemas
Wall in books in journals in letters in newspapers
Wall in sinews in bones in blood in brain cells
And this morning in my own room—

The wall even stretches over two thousand years
From about 200 BC to my laptop
When I click an entry on a foreign website
To read news—

It pops up, unfailingly, engraved with
A motto in Chinese that reads:

Genju xiangguan de falü fagui
Nin suo fangwen de yemian bu yunxu xianshi

'According to relevant policies and laws,
The page you visit is not allowed to display.'

Underwear

James Norcliffe

Deep in the forest the priests
and the secret police are on patrol.

They are so difficult to see among the black branches
and their scurry cannot easily be heard,

although sometimes, just below the wind
and the dripping rain, the tell-tale snap

of a branch will give them away
so that you know they are there.

Their interest, their fascination is underwear:
your underwear: its stains, secretions

and odours and what it tells the state
of the state of your body, your soul.

This knowledge so excites them their fingers flex with it,
stretch with it to part the foliage, their eyes bright

with the possibility that your underwear will
give you away, deliver you completely to them

and they are grateful to your underwear, so grateful
they express their gratitude in files, in trials, in prayers.

PAPA DE LOS POBRES
PERCENTAGES SAY NOT
GAP OF EQUL
RECOGNITION
WOMEN LIVING AT THE BOUNDARIES OF HURT AND GRACE
FANNING HANDS
PILES OF CHORES
RIGHT TO SHELTER
RIGHTS
A STONE IN THE MOUTH
OF THE PEOPLE
CHECK INSPECTOR 29
THIS FLOOR HAS STOLEN MY WRISTS
YOUR EDGES TURN TO DUST
REALLY
TRICKS OF A TREATY
NU TIRANI
Kani te Manukura
PASTURE
TIA F TOTO
MARROW DUST
YOU INSULT MY HOUSE
ARMED OFFENDER
MUD, BLOOD AND BRUTALITY
A BIT FAST
WITCHES
IN
QUEER WING'D PAUSES
LESBOS
WHICH RAPE
SLASHED BY WIND
A WAIST
RAZOR WIRE
FUCK ALL
FUTCHA
DA TRUE LIBERATOR OF AOTEAROA
HINETEIWAIWA (TUTELARY DEITY OF WOMEN AND CHILDBIRTH
TE RAU O TE AROHA
PAPATŪĀNUKU
BOARDED HIS KOHANGA BUS
HE TŪHOE
MAU
NŌ TE UREWERA
KIA WHAKAMANE
NGA WAHINE
DEVIL COMIN DOWN
WE KNOW NO

[PART TWO] RIGHTS

a stone in the mouth of the people

—kani te manukura

Check Inspector 29

Jeffrey Paparoa Holman

I'm a check inspector   check the mine   check the mine
I'm check inspector 29
Check inspector check the mine   check the mine

Back in the year of '67 nineteen died   nineteen died
They changed the law when the miners cried
'We want our men to check the mine!'

I'm a politician making laws   making laws
I'm the Labour Minister I open doors
Big and bigger business knocking at my door   at my door

Check inspectors are miners too   miners too
We're not like him we're one of you   we're one of you
We belong to the working crew   the working crew

Came to the year of '92 a Tory brew   a Tory brew
Came to the House and changed the law   they changed the law
Big and bigger business at their door   at their door

We don't need your check inspectors   check inspectors
We don't need all this red tape   too many too many money brakes
We don't need you any more we'll change the law   change the law

Big and bigger business rubbed their hands   they rubbed their hands
Sang a new song to the working man   the working man
Take it or leave it was the tune they sang   tune they sang

No more no more check inspectors   that was the end of the safe trifecta
Safe trifecta   miner and manager and bureaucrat   safe as houses
Like my old hard hat   my old hard hat you can't beat that

Came to the year of twenty ten   nineteen November was when   was when
Pike River miners put it to the test   put it all to the test
God rest their souls   God rest their souls   29 29 29 souls

Too much methane no way out   big and bigger business too much clout
Too much clout and the corners cut   the corners cut
Risks under pressure   make them a buck   big boss bucks   ran out of luck

An uphill battle when the pit she blew   the pit she blew
No check inspector looking out for you boys   out for you
A check inspector from the miners' crew

The sound of weeping is in the land   she's in the land
From here to China the miners' band   the miners' band
Is dealt that hand   is dealt that hand

Politicians in their beds lying straight and true   straight and true
Never a blink when they say to you   say to you
No idea why the mine she blew   mine she blew

I'm check inspector 29 29 29   I'm check inspector 29
Once I was my brother's keeper   brother's keeper
Now I'm with my sister weeping   sister weeping

Tory ministers bloodstained hands   bloodstained hands
Do-nothing Lefties also rans   also rans
So what the hell is a man is a man   so what the hell is a man?

I'm check inspector 29
Send me back down every mine
Every mine

I won't rest till in my time
I'm back in the mine
Back in the mine

Manufacture

Ivy Alvarez

for Rebecca L

Midday break from factory floor, soles burning with solid
toil, back and forth on concrete. My feet feel deeply soiled.
Dirt or worse, ground in skin. I have my violin. Sweat sticks to my shirt,
soaked with salt. My notes lift us up to forgetting. We nod through cigarette
smoke,
tannic-stained fingers of rust. Stop. Go. I work for my boy. Press down panic:
counter-productive, if I let it. *Prepare.* Every second is a hunter.

More haste. The phrase chases me around the filthy floor,
dim-fingered like a boss, brushing against women. *Trim*
right here, he says, leaning in. Clock-hands point to midnight.
Weigh up overtime shifts, Sunday time and a half, every day
slips, falls. My notes will lift me up—until I break the bowl of my hips.
Think about the small mercy of figs, honey, something to drink,
warm me up. This floor has stolen my wrists. My knees. See? I walk in a
storm
cloud of doubt. Shake my head; time's my friend. Can't get out just yet.

Abrasion

Nigel Brown

The crude process of grinding down
invented by clever dicks
where you work longer hours for less
in the damp and fetid room
of inequality
is not mentioned.

The face on the news
the so-called leader
gets by on platitudes
and shrugs of denial.
Plans your world
in secret.

You are told to run faster.
Swim the polluted rivers.
Told to avoid small gatherings
and not speak to journalists.
Told to shut up about the weather.

In the megastore of cheap
and faulty goods
you are not recognised
unless you buy constantly.
Desire and urges get waved
before you.

Your tiredness is laughed about
by an attitude outside your prison.
Bits of you go missing.
Fall off.
Bit by bit by bit

in the political silence
your edges turn to dust
barely visible.

Boxing Day

Peter Olds

Young people shouldn't have to work
in supermarkets on Boxing Day.
No young person under the age of 35
should have to work during summer
holidays. The owners of supermarkets,

lounging on beach and boat-deck, who
set the whole crazy economy up like it is
in the first place, should be behind
counters and checkouts instead.
Young people should be hitch-hiking across

the country, surfing, getting lost in bush,
making love under waterfalls, rolling
down sand hills—and generally having
a good time (before it's too late), while
the rest of us who love money and

fiddling with our hands, who have been
stupid enough to ignore our own youth,
blindly letting it slip past, who are old,
grey and crotchety—should do all the work …
So—extract yourselves, young ones,
from your Oppressive Checkout Machines

and go and Overthrow a Government or two!
What do you think life is for—the Rich,
the Famous, the Privileged?
Under the *New Republic* no child below
the age of 35 shall be required to work in
supermarkets (or anywhere) on Boxing Day,
if they write poems.

Papa de los pobres (Potatoes of the poor)

Serie Barford

it's the morning after Anzac Day
medals and politics have been aired
with bugles, haka and stylised poppies
marking distant shores, valour and loss

but there are still battles to be had in the suburbs

where the recession's struck a hunch-backed woman
in jandals, trackpants and a budget-rack floral parka

she's braked a pushchair chocker with chokos
on the pavement outside Countdown

when I close in on her I see she's fine-boned
that her misshapen back is actually a papoose
slung beneath a mantle of synthetic flowers

and there are bald patches around the hood
where tiny fists have plucked nylon fur
to suck for warmth in the Autumn wind

the woman holds a shard of corrugated card
her smile as shaky as the crayoned lettering
$1 a choko
her face is gentle
undemanding

but I have chokos galore at home
their wrinkled, prickly flesh a green chorus
with feijoas and fresh figs in a pottery bowl

and I need four gold coins for the special toothpaste
guaranteed to sooth receded gums and nerves

the papoose whimpers

I pluck two fruit from the sagging canvas shelf
extract gold coins from my purse
smile then wince when the wind targets my mouth

this is for the chokos
and these are for your child

she shakes her head
no no
takes one coin
presses the others back into my palm

I mean well but I've got it all wrong
she lifts her chin

I left my island for a better life

another woman approaches
scoops up chokos
papa de los pobres! she exclaims

she sees a woman with empty cupboards
who's taken to the streets to change things

stands to attention
salutes the urban activist

Percentages

Benita H. Kape

I can still smell the sweet river loam,
dark and full of goodness. Bitterness
tainting as I held my own and sometimes
more. I was not to be beaten by the frost
or my brother and his two friends, and
this, I knew, was one of the reasons I'd
been chosen: though I'll grant there were
few others available or, to my brother,
doubtless proven to this arduous task. So
we worked and we fooled that autumn,
just started high school; wiry, stubborn,
thirteen going on fourteen years old.

End of first school term saw me bent over,
bagging those potatoes, hauling heavy sacks,
hefting for a local farmer the full two weeks.
And I followed my brother as he dug the row,
hour by cruel frosty hour in May.

No agreed wages, and I doubt very much
my brother and his friends had negotiated.
Came the day I was handed an envelope; one
pound and ten shillings it contained (three
dollars in today's exchange though the
value rated greater over time). But still
it was half that paid to this cocky brother
of mine. Had he cheated me? Part of me
knew he had not. But someone had! It
burned and grew as attitudes remained
into my adult years. I knew my worth
equal to any, a simple fact. I came
through the hard school.

Another thirty years down the line,
intent upon change, I was there for the
conferences, marches, placards!
Among many things I wanted equal pay.

May, the frosts set in. My blood rises.
I take sustenance from frosts, digging
my small urban plot; age beginning
to overtake me. The winter of my life
presupposes a better outcome, so that still
I plunge into the old spud of an argument:
have we yet narrowed the gap of equal
recognition; parity and pay?
Percentages say not.

Cabin fever

Nell Barnard

The ceiling is dust-white,
crowded with the memory of spiders

Here below, we read a pile of children's books
their pages brittle in the winter air

It is so cold some nights, the heater is like a toy

I dress my small son in a thick wool sweater
handmade, fur-brown with buttons
I can afford just one

I think of women living
at the boundaries of hurt and grace,
feeding their children on cobwebs and dreams

We are not so different
from each other

The mystic tells us all shall be well
but the goddess of adjustment chimes in: '*feel, choose …*'

What is good will warm you
like the sun

Winter coast

Nicola Easthope

So far, the old house holds.
Communication lines pull the gable south—
face into the squall, taut to the pole
as rigging in open sea. Macrocarpa falls for fire
stoke, powerless at the roots. Oil fins betray
fanning hands; no fire to boil. Hat and mittens
help sleep. The window glass sucks in
and out, candle heads tossing.
Wool and cold worry will carry us
into the long forecasted more.

Chores

Judith Stanley

Today
I have done the dishes
hung a tub of clean washing
cooked and fed
scrubbed the sink
vacuumed the space
and dusted
I have listened to the radio
and heard a broadcast of events
while peeling potatoes
and note
the Minister for Household Duties
did not legislate
against the endless piles of chores
nor seek funds for the garden to grow
and I have found time to sit and survey
the clean room
and thought
the child did well
to put her crayons away
before standing on them.

Entitlement

Melanie McKerchar

You have the right to say no.
You have the right to freedom of association, movement, peaceful assembly.
You have the right to free speech.
You have the right to remain silent.

You have the right to refuse treatment, not to be experimented on or
tortured.
You have the right not to be deprived of life.
You do not have the right to health, to be pain free, to be free of mental
torment.
You do not have the right to die.

You have the right to education, leisure, to drink and smoke, to fight for
your country.
You have the right to vote, or to abstain.
You have the right to be right, left, centre, red, blue, green, rainbow.
You have the right to belief, to worship your chosen god/prophet/deity/
healer/shaman.
You do not have the right to happiness, a job, a house, a car, a big-screen TV.

You have the right to marry any person of legal age you choose.
You have the right to divorce them.
You have the right to 50 per cent of their stuff.
They have the right to 50 per cent of your stuff.
You do not have the right to love.

You do not have the right to shelter.
You do not have the right to money.
You do not have the right to friends, lovers or freedom from ridicule.
You have the right to remain silent.
You do not have the right to die.
You have the right to remain silent.

My dad loves the All Blacks

Jessie Fenton

Okay, I know that's not a very exciting way to start a poem. I mean, every dad loves the All Blacks. It's on the list of Mandatory Dad Things to Love, along with bacon, beer, and responding to 'I'm hungry' with 'Hi Hungry, I'm Dad!'

But, my dad *loves* the All Blacks. My dad loves the All Blacks like owning every shirt they've ever played in.
My Dad loves the All Blacks like when my brother took up soccer in sixth form, I got a rugby ball for Christmas.
My dad loves the All Blacks like sending me drunk selfies from Twickenham Stadium.

And I … didn't watch the World Cup final.

I know, I'm sorry. I had a law exam the next day, okay?

Instead, I stayed up all night reading up on battered women's syndrome. That's a legal term for a woman who succumbs to 'learned helplessness', to a relationship so embroiled in fists and fear and fierce love she can no longer claw her way out of it.

And as my flatmates down the hall cheered for Dan Carter's latest kick,

I wondered what it says about us as a country that we have to invent a whole new syndrome to explain what we do to our women.

What does it mean when the only people happier than my dad that the All Blacks won were the women who didn't have to hide from those fists that night?

What does it mean when we can forgive a man for breaking a woman's back because he shares such good rugby memes on Facebook?

What does it mean when the only models we have for manhood come from mud, and blood, and brutality, from the boys in black to Gallipoli, as if the only way to be a man is through brute force?

And I love the All Blacks. This is not about them. This is about us. Because Richie is a hero, but—

Julian Savea is not.

Tony Veitch is not.

I am so sick of us making mountains out of men who act like avalanches, measuring their manhood by how many women's bodies they can bury beneath them.

As if my dad wasn't most man when he cried the whole way through *Les Mis* with me. When he came to hear my poetry, and through every mention of pubic hair and penetration he didn't flinch once.
And I didn't flinch once, while watching the rugby with him.

Because I know how much of a man he is.

The speed of God

Rhian Gallagher

What if God had slowed down after making the grass and the stars and the whales and let things settle for a bit so the day could practise leaving into the arms of the night and the tides tinker their rhythms and the stars find their most dramatic positions.

Or maybe if he'd made man and said, 'You learn how to live with yourself and do housework and then I might think about woman.'

Or instead he'd made woman not out of a rib, which was really such a last resort, but rising out of the firmament, one woman followed by more women, and they took journeys and learnt how to build boats and bridges which surely they would have done without men around pushing and shoving and constantly giving orders.

I just think it was a bit fast—six days to make all of it. How could the relationship between things be seen, be felt? And really, the whole of so-called civilisation has been trying to figure it out ever since.

And as if God's rush were in us too we go about remodelling faster and faster with our burning and breaking and the loss mounts up against the new—faster and faster and the earth reels with our speed and it looks and feels like a disaster.

Pink

Martha Morseth

A rainbow doesn't have pink I tell her
if God wanted girls to wear that colour
you'd see it in the sky.

Fingering each rack with disappointment
she rejects a blue top, a skirt in purple
even a belt of sparkles and gold.

Grandma, you don't understand
everyone has pink
Barbie has a pink car and shoes.

Pink is weak, silly and girlie, I grumble
you need a colour that shows your strength
a royal blue or brilliant yellow.

She leads me to the teen department
a field of sequined and shiny black leather.
Witches are strong, she says and grins.

A late take on the Marriage Amendment Act

Heather Avis McPherson

The First Poets I shut with a wry grin, reminded of horny peeping
toms who used to ask what lesbians do in bed—and here I'm
thumbing through dozens of lusty males doing lusty
bed things—mostly to each other—to fossick out
the She who wrote: *some men say an army of horse—foot—ships—*
is the most beautiful thing on earth—but I say it's what
you love—and Sappho sings the lovely Anaktoria. Or Gongyla.

Or others. And for singing against war—and the military in charge—
the Tyrant exiles her to Sicily—and gets toppled. Now scholars
piece her words out of mummy-cloth papyrus since all
whole poems but one and all her music's lost. What
of Corinna of Tanagra? Never! It's Sappho of Eressus
who fetches hordes to Lesbos—global Amazons *whose wild*
shenanigans dismay the villagers and face tut-tuttery on
the beaches—and are not as troublous as the refugees
who flee their tyrants' wars and drown in Sappho's waters.

Sappho—mocked, banned, lost, forgotten—loved women much too
much and too deliciously to turn them back or stay a wife—
while the Corinna who says *women shouldn't*—
we shrug off as any bossy collaborative sister
who scolds us for being too feminist, too lesbian
and not lining up behind the blokes—or for sailing between
Scylla & Charybdis and not getting swept into whirlpools or
crashing on rocks in somebody else's heaving sea of identity and needs.

Some claim Sappho leapt off a cliff for love of a ferryman youth. Rubbish!
A made-up myth! They hate her loving women. She boasts a beloved
child, grieves that one of her favourites is marrying the luckiest
of men, sends a plea to laughing Aphrodite to bless her
latest love—*O Sappho, not again*—she sings

at weddings, scolds an adulterous brother, flourishes
a hymn-board of her lovers, is honoured beside Homer, cherished
by poets and women—especially those who love and marry other
women—so let's—if we survive the planet hotting up, floods
bigger than Noah's, disasters larger than Nagasaki,
Fukushima or lethally free-ranging religios, politicos, drones—

let's do the Sapphic living we dream in queer wing'd pauses
under the trees—in gardens circling Western Springs
Park where geese—swans—eels—gulls—coots—
pūkeko—rabbits—and ducks—married or not—
co-exist consummately in couples and families and flocks.

Talking about rape

Ruth Hanover

when I got back—it was a dormitory—
I showered
used disinfectant
meant
for the floors

in terms of evidence
this,
was a mistake

when I got back here
a friend of a friend asked
was he Black?
which leads me to the
problem
in talking about rape—
which is
that you might not even begin to
comprehend
which rape
I am
referring to

From the house where he took her life

Johanna Aitchison

'I gave him his footsteps,'
said the stairs to her upstairs.

'I gave him five sharp knocks
on my door,' said her bedroom.

'I gave him all of my metal,'
said the lock on her door.

'I gave him her arms floating out
towards him,' said her open suitcase.

'I gave him her striped curtains,
her photos tacked to wallpaper,

the silver light shining
from her computer screen,

I gave him her trees, slashed
by wind outside her window,

I gave him blackbirds,
screaming off the power lines,

I gave him the chipped marble
waves of her harbour view,' said the house.

Stomach it

Amy Paulussen

my stomach is so much more
than the organ of that name
what I mean is
all the stuff between my ribs
and my pubes
all the workings I need
for important things
like a glass of wine after a long day
a toasted sandwich for a lazy dinner
and all the coffee I down
between jobs
and I've a uterus
in good working condition
though I'm done with it
and want it safely tied off
so that all it can do is keep my hormones in check
no small thing
and then there are muscles,
stronger than they look
thanks to carrying kids up steps and hills
cheese and bread and wine
hide those good abs
and fill out my skin
lined by remnants of tans
and clothes
and babies
silvery trails like a whole family of snails
marked their path
soft to the touch
like bruised apple
suck it in
as if lesser is better

my kingdom for a waist
trumps function
unless I can find the gumption
to wear this spare tyre
like a man does
proud of what he contains

Arohata

Janis Freegard

You wait in the car, then outside the first gate,
then go through to the next gate where a woman
tells you to hurry because it won't open
until the first one's safely closed behind you;

you get the feeling she's a regular here,
she knows the drill; you thank her, pass quickly through,
exit the second gate together, wonder
what comes next; you've tried to dress respectably

so you don't get searched or barred, you don't want to
make trouble for your friend while she's in this place.
Inside, you watch what everyone else does while
queuing; you place the books on the metal tray

to be inspected by the woman behind
the glass; you see now you should have brought them in
a plastic bag marked with your friend's name like the
woman in front of you did & you make a

mental note to do that next time you visit;
you already know you can't bring her chocolate
or cigarettes, just phone cards & things to read
& you could have brought money but you brought books.

Meantime your friend's been waiting in an airtight
room for over half an hour, waiting in her
orange suit that almost glows; they're all in there
breathing in silence, careful not to panic

because there's not enough air for it & soon
they'll have to look upbeat & entertaining
yeah it's not so bad in here, then afterwards
they'll be strip searched. When you see your friend you're not

supposed to touch her, but the wardens don't stop
a quick hug, so that's good, and you have to sit
in the right seat, not the prisoner seat which
is a different colour; your friend says the food's

good but someone rolled her room; you hear about
that woman they said stood by & watched a rape
& the one who failed to save her baby when
her partner beat it to death; your friend says she's

not all there, that one. Outside, the high fence is
topped with razor wire & the obligatory
singing blackbird; you walk back out through the gates
to the car, breathing. Breathing the wide, wide sky.

tricks of a treaty

kani te manukura

article the first:
one good trick, that one
played by empire
on our tīpuna
how could they have known
by making their mark
on that paper
we, the descendants of chiefs
would become palimpsest
upon the pages of this land
the signs of our
past present future
made so faint
we can barely see our own shadows
let alone that of the land
as both pass to the pākehā
upon whom the sun never
seems to set

stories that carried us safely
across space & time
now told by simple strangers
climb pine trees
upside down torn apart
by bush lawyer vine

it's fuck all really
but let my every word
be a stone in the mouth of the people
for those who do not know
the purposes of a pebble
at least it will help shut you up

for those who do
hold it long under your tongue
he mea hāpai ō:
provisions for the journey

because of the tricks of a treaty
we gotta long way to go

article the second:
you, the ran'atira
wo/men of great mana
have the choice of signing
or not signing
this trick of a treaty
with a mere messenger
distinguished from the rest of the syphilitic sailors
& crude whalers
only by his fancy dress
& the title it entails

they aren't even giving you the respect
of trying to cover their tracks:
you know what
a hobson's choice is, ay?

no?
oh, you're gonna have one good laugh at this …

article the third:
if your bent is more political-economic
you will sign thinking,
only the shadow of the land
will pass to the strangers
the substance will remain
let the queen govern for a time
we will trade potato pig flour
& grow our material power

if your bent is more spiritual-metaphysic
you will sign thinking
only the substance of the land
will pass to the strangers
but the shadow will remain
let the queen govern for a time
we will maintain the mana to guide her hand
and the stories that bind us to the land

either way you will be wrong

for the trick of a treaty
made with an empire
upon whom, for a time at least,
the sun never set
is both substance & shadow
the strangers will get

article the fourth:
the truest trick
of a treaty
is to offer a lot
then
to the promises of paper
supply an antidote
bring it in by the boat

call it commerce,
call it provision of goods & services
according to the natural laws
of supply & demand
aw heck,
go the full farce & call it a civilising mission

don't worry
the natives will give this powerful potion
one good name

something like,
karaitianatan'a
kai papa
or waipiro

whatever you or they call it
be sure
to dress it in red
that way
it'll go straight to their head

article the fifth:
among all the other mystical reasons
is this one:
you will sign believing

hei wakaritenga mai hoki tenei mo te wakaaetanga ki te kawanatanga o te kuini—ka tiakina e te kuini o ingarani nga tangata maori katoa o nu tirani
ka tukua ki a ratou nga tikanga katoa rite tahi ki ana mea ki nga tangata o ingarani

possesses sufficient authority moral weight
to protect your people
from syphilitic sailors whalers rapists rapacious missionaries
assorted riff raff
thrown to the farthest margins of empire

no one will admit just yet
the difference between
the ones transporting & those transported
is mere money power class
that is to say,
smoke, mirrors,
a simple trick of light

what you learn,
that a treaty signed with gangsters
is no kind of treat at all,
will not even provide a fig leaf
to cover your losses
even worse
hindsight will continually tell you
the lesson
has not been well learnt

article the sixth:
so clever of you
to not teach the natives
your tongue
before they signed
i mean, that way
how could they see the
double-crossed-cultural entendre
of 'nu tirani'

surely no accident
it sounds so similar to
new tyranny

anglican prattle

Vaughan Rapatahana

compelled to attend
this cross-high byre
every sacrosanct sunday,
lined up to listen to
a blubber & blither
of blustery bullshit
on repentance, remission,
omission & missions;

ultimate delivery
fed out as forage
for our souls
imploring redemption;
reserving, deserving
to be trucked upwards
via winged chariots
to pledged halls of fame.

clasping old hymnals
like they were electric,
pages of gibberish
faded in hope,
singing in lines
like synchronised swimmers
wolfing down wafers
& stagnant red wine.

listening to sermons
staining our sins,
an obloquy of ordure
from the lips of a jester
dressed across gender
bovine-eyed herds
smiling in lies

while we shook
shaking hands
of choleric clergy;
this pareidolia
of pawns, or peon
to the slaughter?

god, no need for this
deliberate evasion;
just lead us to pasture,
to seek our own succour,
we don't wish to be fed
such anglophile drivel,
we won't pray for glib penance,

which steers us
to
some sort of communion
with these white waves and ways.

The quickest way to trap a folktale

Mere Taito

a research institution walks into a village
                    scholarly clothes
                    sharp alien tools
fine-spun birthmarks flow out of a magic twig
a wet metallic nose presses onto the thinnest
white flat bread that folds into a boat

a research institution gets to work
it asks us to open our mouths
we open
it lifts our tongues and prods
we sit very still
it pinches our uvulae with its forefinger and thumb
we do not gag
it pokes its head in and calls up to our nasal cavities
'hello, is anyone up there?'
'hello?'
we do not sneeze it out of our conscience
it holds a light into our eyes
we do not blink

a research institution collects its treasures
Mafi and Lu's marriage
annulled in a gazebo of hard covers
Raho's canoe
chopped and chiselled to stand like an antique spine
Moeatiktiki's congealed birth
moulded into an impractical jacket
Kirkirsasa's armpit tattoos
transfused into an overbearing gothic title
Tinrau's bird
taxidermised into a pretentious Preface

Puaknifo and Mostoto's fists
bloodied in Volume IX Footnote 8
Tiaftoto's oyster shell
shucked in a gloating Afterword

a research institution walks out of a village
boards its white flat bread boat
scholarly clothes
the sharpest alien tool
Copyright ©

Whenua ghosts

Ria Masae

Did you know native bones are
buried across the bay?
Do the holidaymakers you entice
with wine trails know they sip
marrow-dust of the dead?
When you lure them
with brochures of en-gulf waters
do they know they swim
in the salt of ancestral blood?

Do new settlers realise they tread
on the front line between
baptism and blasphemy?
Will the redevelopment schemes
leashed to your cash-collar
buy your forgiveness
when the haka rains from the sky
on the cusp of Justice delivered?

Are you denying the bones
beneath brown skins
have always been
as white as yours
and we are all reduced to
grey ash in the end?

Speaking rights

Anahera Gildea

My neighbour is learning te reo. Man he's proud
of his long body of white
flicking hair, conquering language. He doesn't feel
an inch of guilt. Nothing. He feels nothing. Man he's proud.
I've learned my mihi, he says,
where you say your mountain and stuff. He struts
and tells me his mang-ga. Then his moan-a.
He can tell me where *I'm* from too
he's found a site
that can trace my whakapapa for me. Shit that's good.
It's all just on the internet now. Your iwi all the way back
to your waka.
Man, he's proud. Do you know poi e? he says.
Prince what's his name. The big guy. You'd like it.

Manaakitanga mutes my thunder,
my eyes wide, short stepping him out of my whare
frightening the fuck out of him, beating
my drums at him. Who do you think you are?
How dare you?
You butcher me. Still,
two hundred years on you insult my house,
pissing your kōrero everywhere.
You represent no one, and nothing
when you speak.

When I speak, my pepeha
is standing
is anchored
to speak with the consent of every single one of my ancestors;
she who nursed koroua through the pākehā fever,
he who married the forbidden,

she who plunged into the rapids to rescue children,
they who carried their pou, from hīkoi to hīkoi
across the motu
so we could speak, I speak, I call,
to the mountain that forged shelter for us,
the ground beneath that remembers every breath
loved here, lost here, fighting
right at your fucking feet.
Their blood the stratum that reaches forward into the future,
accumulating, hardening, speeding
into this exact moment,
into this very person who matters,
it matters what she says, it makes a difference every time,
not throw away, not nothing,
not ever alone.
I am held up, infused, risk taking
with the strength of a thousand hands
who demand, shout or whisper, that I dig in my toes,
that I make them proud.

If I do they surround me,
words, thoughts, hearts,
swell, swell up behind me, feet askance,
bodies wide open to the sky,
voices harmonising in waiata that resound, rise,
rise up,
no longer silent, the bones of Papatūānuku
afford speaking rights to all.

So, good on you, man, for learning the reo.
You must be proud.

For those of you who insist on using the term Te Urewera 17, 12 or 4 to accompany any newspaper headline or media soundbite

Maraea Rakuraku

Te Urewera 1 is 20 kms from Whakatane, 65 kms southwest from Rotorua along state highway 38, 32 kms from Opotiki, 63 from Wairoa, 40 minutes from Kawerau, two hours from Rotorua, five hours from Auckland and seven hours 635 kms and a timewarp away from the life I lead in Wellington.
Te Urewera 2 is Ruātoki, Waiohau, Ruatāhuna, Te Waimana and Waikaremoana. It is not Kutarere, Kawerau, Tāneatua, Murupara or a national park.
Te Urewera 3 is Tūhoe.
Te Urewera 4 is a kuia shocked that Māori pay for their watercress and pūhā from the Hainamana down the road when there is some across the fence in the paddock, over there.
Te Urewera 5 is a bum wiggling, eyes googling and tongue swinging on television screens, Every. Single. Time. The iwi is mentioned.
Te Urewera 6 is a 15-year-old girl who sleeps sitting up fully clothed in her bed which lies across the doorway of her bedroom, with the open window within jumping distance, and knives in the door jamb.
Te Urewera 7 is a father pining for a son he hasn't seen in 20 years.
Te Urewera 8 is a lawyer working her arse off on the raupatu, trying to get the best deal for her people with a tāne undermining her every move.
Te Urewera 9 is a nine-year-old kid who still mimi's the bed because when he was five, the Armed Offenders boarded his kōhanga bus.
Te Urewera 10 is a whānau in Australia making their biennial pilgrimage back for Te Hui Ahurei a Tūhoe.
Te Urewera 11 is a boy asking what the (moo-teh) mute button on the TV does.
Te Urewera 12 are artists graffitiing under the Onehunga Bridge—Te Mana Motuhake ō Tūhoe.
Te Urewera 13 are at Te Tirahou waiting for the tupāpaku to arrive before they accompany the whānau back to Ruātoki, Waiohau, Ruatāhuna, Maungapohatu, Te Waimana or Waikaremoana.

Te Urewera 14 are the many learning te reo Māori and reconnecting with their Tūhoetanga.

Te Urewera 14 are the many who are not.

Te Urewera 15 is the aunty who orders the whānau to empty their kai from their freezers and bring it to the pā when a whānau from Christchurch turns up with a tupāpaku no one knows. And no money.

Te Urewera 16 is the whānau waiting at the gate, whakamā about walking onto the pā bringing back the mate of their koro who left 40 years ago and never came home.

Te Urewera 17 are those at te hau kāinga tending the flame and burning the fires so we always find our way home.

Te Urewera 18 are those of us who live away from home due to circumstance and choice.

They are not kaupapa-hijacking opportunists who through the skinniest of links arrogantly associate themselves with a cause, a people, a way of life that is here forever and will be, long after they move on to their next cause.

They do not privilege themselves over the historical pain of 40,000 Tūhoe.

He Tūhoe ahau, nō Te Urewera.

In her own words

Sandi Hall

Poor by marriage the pākehā wāhine
robbed of land and power by it
leaving them trivial
as bunnies on a baby's bib.
Wāhine Māori keep the whenua
of their birth, regardless
who they wed. I would tell you
mine but a kūmara does not speak
of its own sweetness.

I can say I am the great grand
daughter of Nga-kahu-whero, and
daughter of Re Te Tai, Te Rarawa
chief in the Hokianga, where
blue pūkeko
legs step redly in the reeds.

At eighteen, I wed Hāmiora
Mangakāhia of Ngāti Whanaunga,
his third wife and, he says, best.
Now I am Meri Te Tai Mangakāhia.
Hami likes my young body hot

in his bed, fingers deft
and supple, musical he says
from the piano I play.

My puku bulging with our first,
Hami returns from a meeting—
Te Kotahitanga is born!
He is full of it, how Māori
must have our own parliament,

govern our own affairs, as
who can trust pākehā
to do right by us?
'Will wāhine be members of Kotahitanga?'
I asked Hami. His eyebrows flew up
but, 'Ask them,' he finally says.

To be first is as hard as a baby's head
pushing the pelvis apart;
our third was still invisible when I saw
five pīwakawaka flying
on Whatipu Marae as I gave
my solemn karere:

'E whakamoemiti atu ana ahau …
ko te take i mōtini atu ai ahau,
ki te Tumuaki Hōnore, me nga mema

hōnore, kia mahia he ture e tēnei whare
kia whakamana nga wāhine, ki te pooti mema
mo ratou ki te Pāremata Māori.'*

I felt my own words clothing
me in power, right
as a chiefly cloak. Even though
false Akenehi Tomoana sliced at the
root of my motion, the idea lived.

In the end her slash was useless,
a paper gun. With wāhine
women together
the vote was won

---

* *Translation*: I move this motion before the honourable leader and all honourable members so that a law may emerge from this parliament to allow women to vote and women to be accepted as members of the Māori parliament.

Shakespeare on Lorne

Carin Smeaton

Featuring:
Mister Buttons as Mister Buttons
Ranginui as da open sky
Papatūānuku as the beautiful earth
Tāne Mahuta as a sneeze maker
Tama-nui-te-rā as da eva glorious sun
Daleks as da ladies and gentlemens

shakespeare's high on lorne street on the second floor in the quiet room
the glass one wit no apps up an escalator on the left where a man in a suit
of buttons (called buttons) dozes away wit his head hangin off da edge
wondrin how his children gonna grow up wit da dollars vaping away on
da rents n ntensification inhalin nostril high throughout the city (like
through a tru blu bong) lingering over nuku in the lazy light of an
evenin-sky-sly-sun due to be settin round now but instead rā jus gettin
ready 4 da rub lubricatin his westie rays (four winds warm) wit his spirit
fingers spiritin away some noisy flat-white know-it-all ladies n gents
who is spillin their thermal breaths all over da show (like some split open
legs) in the shakespeare room and frankly button's gettin tired of hearing
bout their festival plans their property do-ups their solar-or-nots (shootin
up karma like they is squirrels on speed) makin him cough open the old
books bout melancholy tellin you jus how sadness actually is (how it'll
cut youse down deadly in half or in quarters or into eighths like a tudor)
and how youse better get better wit a warm dose of warm lafs n musik
tick tick ticklin away at da earth like how tāne mahuta does sneezin da
life into whatever the devil's comin down goin on goin up

Ah Tonto … watcha gonna do 'bout Aotearoa?

Reihana Robinson

we on da brink boy
we know no futcha
we aint got our own lingo
we talk Americano
wanna be like you Tonto
wan da big horse
wan da big land
wan to be da star of yo movie

how you gonna come down heya
liberate our loser mom and pops
sweet-talk our girlfrens?
all our sistas are jus waitin
fo yo hunk o flesh
all our sistas suck in der fat bellies
make goggle eyes at yo cartoon
are ready to make peace man

dat look in yo eye
dat sage breath
dat lithium skin
dat tribal paint job
all if it will work down heya
just steam yo way
beam yo way
triumph on horseback
we know no animosity
we like injuns
but maybe you oughta bring along
dat cowboy jus in case

wen da winds blow hard
over da southern skies
mounted police look good on postcards
we welcome you and yo brudda
we give up our seat for you brudda
we taunt our officers in da knowledge
you are comin brudda
you are what gives us fever
we eat only pūhā and kōura

for dis second coming
will raise us from da dead
we will shine like movie stars
radiate da magazine covers
we will ululate wid ghost-like voices
to freak out da mudda penetrators
to buy back to make free hold
all da trees and da birds so we can
be free man
free man, yeah, you can make dis happen
you carry all da wise words of yo nation
you fill da hearts full hope
you are da true liberator
of Aotearoa

come on man
make it happen

Aue

Zoe Taptiklis

Ko [insert name] tōku ingoa
Ko [hill/mountain] te maunga
Ko [renamed transliterally] te awa
Ko [pre-colonial] te iwi
Ko [this land is now a mall] te marae
Ko Honda Civic te waka
Ko Adam Smith te tangata o te waka
Ko pōwhiri a rūnanga pākehā

I am [insert name]
[hill/mountain] is my mountain
[renamed transliterally] is my river
[pre-colonial] is my family's heritage
[this land is now a mall] is our home
I came in a Honda Civic
Adam Smith drove the car
This is the introduction of the white person

Ko Ora tōku ingoa
Ko Hikurangi te maunga
Ko Waiapu te awa
Ko Horouta te waka
Ko Paua tangata o te waka
Ko Ngāti Porou te iwi
Ko Iretekura, ko Kiekie a ko Taharora tōku marae
Ko pōwhiri a rūnanga pākehā

*Life** *is my name*
Hikurangi is my mountain
Waiapu is my river
Horouta is the boat that brought us here
Paua captained this boat
Ngāti Porou is this tribe
We gather at Iretekura, Kiekie and Taharora
This is the introduction of a white person

Ko blonde girl! Hey! You girl! ahau
Ko toilet (brown on the inside, white on the outside) te iwi
Ko watch me change with the land
We are growing without you
And if the land I stand on is falling to the ocean

Blonde girl! Hey! You girl! Is my name
Toilet, brown on the inside, white on the outside, is where I am from
Watch me change with the land

* Zoe is the Greek for Life, and Ora is my Māori name. A transliteration is Roe.

Let its salt and its seething dissolve
me
Submerge these bodies
Never turn your back to Tangaroa

Aue Rona,
Kei runga ra, te marama e whiti
ana*
Marama, gripping me in his fist of
sleep,
Grinning and you're left to wonder
what Rona told him
—When we're sleeping
We're not so different—

Alas Rona,
It's up there, the risen moon

'How's that then, eh? … She's a
cheeky girl.'

* Lyrics from the waiata 'Aue Rona': http://folksong.org.nz/rona/

Poems promoting peace*

Aroha Yates-Smith

Karanga†

Horahia te takapau
o Hine-te-iwaiwa
hei moenga tamariki,
hei nohoanga wānanga
kia tau ai te rongo-ā-marae
te mauri e!

Lay down the ceremonial mat of Hine-te-iwaiwa
as a safe sleeping space for children,
a place for discussions,
ensuring that peace reigns
and life's essence is secured.

~

Waiata‡

Pā kino mai te hau aitū
ki te kiri o te tangata,
ki te wairua o te ao nei.
He hau mate te hau o Tū.

---

* While described here as poems, the lyrics of these karanga, waiata and haka have additional functions located within a Māori context. They were composed for a feature documentary entitled *Tau Te Mauri Breath of Peace*.

† The words of the karanga are delivered by a woman with appropriate skills. Hine-te-iwaiwa is a tutelary deity of women and childbirth.

‡ This waiata or sung poem is a response to the French tests in Mururoa. The wind of misfortune (radioactive fallout) strikes humankind (literally 'the person's skin') and the world's wairua (spirit). The wind of Tū (Tūmatauenga—a war god) portends death. The stance of the people demonstrates that the practice of killing people—haehae tāngata (literally lacerating people)—must cease. Rather, one should proffer the symbol of peace (te rau o te aroha—the leaf of love and compassion) as an offering to Papatūānuku, Mother Earth.

Te tū a te iwi ki te whakaatu e,
me mutu te haehae tāngata.
Hōmai te rau o te aroha
hei takoha ki a Papa e.

The ill wind, the wind of misfortune
strikes the people
and the spiritual essence of this world.
The breath of Tū is a harbinger of death and misfortune.

People rise and make a stand,
that the killing must cease.
Offer, instead, the leaf of love, a token of peace,
a gift to Papa.

~

Haka*

Whakarongo! Whakarongo!
Whakarongo mai rā
koutou, ngā taurekareka
e takahi nei
i te mana tangata,
mana whenua,
mana taiao e.

Kāti rā te kōhuru
i ngā mokopuna,
tūkino i ngā moutere
o te Moana-nui-ā-Kiwa e!
Aue! Aue! Aue hi!

* As with 'Pā kino mai', the words of this haka (postural dance) proclaim the need for people of power to employ more peaceful means of living in this world.

Listen! Listen!
Hear us, you scoundrels
who trample the mana,
the spiritual essence of humankind,
of the land and Nature,
the environment at large.

Listen! Take heed!
You must stop murdering our grandchildren
and destroying islands
of the Pacific Ocean.
Enough is enough! Aue! Aue! Aue hi!

Dis-Oriental Bay

Trevor Hayes

Have I missed the train
To Mumbai? Where is my
Opium? Is that a golden
Buddha reclining?
There is a Gulf of Siam
Between us, man, as, dazed
And confused after a wee
Siesta, I catch
Your easy racism
Taking its dog for a walk.
That's the problem, you say,
With Oriental Bay, too many
Of 'em … Ha Ha Fucking Hilarious!
You should have been a comedian.
Should have been a poet.
Should have been a Taoist mountain
Hermit laughing at the grasshopper's
Lack of sincerity. Should have
Collected firewood daily.
You should have sailed down the Ganges,
The Indus, the Yellow, the Mekong rivers.
You should have invented fireworks.
Should have defended your country
From foreign invaders. Should have
Moved to the city in search of employment.
Should have loved your wife and children.
Should have cried because someone you loved died.
You should have sat alone in the void.
Seriously, you really should have.

Occupy Dunedin

Alison Denham

Spring comes late after the slow
rising and flowering of daffs and tulips.
If some of the chrysalis sleeping bags
are empty, their denizens drying out their
wings under some heatpump somewhere,
it seems no massive deceit.

The little eruptions of tents and plethora
of mixed messages, a lunchtime face to
talk to, the responsibility of it—no open fire
in a public domain, rotating the tents and
scattering grass seed where groundsheets
have put an end to photosynthesis.
Greedy ducks come and eat free seed.

Cold quiet small camp like a lump in the throat,
a disquiet occupying the area around the heart.

Waimakariri and the hikoi

Kathleen Gallagher

The walkers from Bluff
cross the Waimakariri at dusk
the sky huge red
the sun
the rain
the nineteen days
burned in their faces
in their bones

this way of walking hollows out the soul
makes it wide open to the wind and sky
the soles of the feet cry
into the land
this walking in trust
in prayer
from the tail of the fish
to the tongue
from the heel of the waka
to the prow
an opening up of the land
of the people
of the Spirit

everywhere the sound of shoe on gravel on tar
on soft dry grass
carrying the pain
of the shifting of wealth to a tiny minority
in the space of twelve slim years
the increase in poverty of the great majority
unable now to afford a doctor, a dentist, the milk
the kids' shoes, the stamp on a letter to a friend in mourning

these are the places
where the feet meet the ground and echo
this is the poverty, talking, walking
rubbing against the dry stony parts of the island
carrying the pain of the people
upward and outward
across the islands
through the air
breaking the silence
flaming out like this huge red sun above the alps

First thing

Lynley Edmeades

On Twitter this morning
a writer is criticising a politician
who is criticising another politician
for criticising Eleanor Catton.

Tomorrow, it's a story in the *NZ Herald*.
You do things like that
when you become fully grown, things
other people read about first thing.

It rains, then stops, and then
rains again. I can hear the rain
making small miracles in the ground.

Of all those seeds you've planted
some will become fully grown
and some simply won't.

Every day my name is out there

Diane Brown

Some say it's pointless, we have no say
but every day they land in my inbox
or on Facebook, petitions asking
for my name: on state housing,
refugees, the TPPA, the writers
imprisoned for telling the truth,
the stoning of adulteress women,
the rising of the seas,
the whales choking on plastic,
the starving in Ethiopia
(always the starving in Ethiopia).
Today there will be calls asking
to support the banning of pitbulls
after yet another mauling.
No question, I do the right thing
the liberal left, right thing,
enter my email address,
press send, there's a satisfying woosh
like a kererū winging overhead.
It's out there, my name
in the ether, and I get back to doing
what I do, as if I've been to confession,
cleansed myself of the world's woes
and sins. A brief moment
of engagement, painless.
The point is, I've let the angels
know I'm on their side.

IN THE FUTURE
ENVIRONMENT
TAKING
SELFIES BY THE RUINS
WE COLLECT THE KORIMAKO
REVIGORISE THE CAPITAL GAIN
THE DRILL WORKING NOW ON THAT WATER UNDER GROUND
YOU CONTROL IT ALL
A LOT OF POST COLONIAL DIRT
NO ARTICLE OF FAITH
JUST EXCREMENT
JETSAM ON THE TIDE
I KEPT PICKING UP THE TRASH
THERE'S NO CLIMATE CHANGE
HIGH TIDES SEEP INTO THE GARDEN
APE SHIT GO
SEE THE SHORT-HAIRED APES
AWAITING THE GULP OF A NEW LONG CENTURY
LET THE GARDEN CITY RECLAIM ITS NAME
TIDES TOO HIGH TOO OFTEN
BABYLON IS
STORM COMING, BEYOND OUR KNOWLEDGE OF STORM!
VEXING TUSSOCK
WE ARE MILLIONS
STOATS
WATER
IRRIGATORS
N Brown 2016

[PART THREE] ENVIRONMENT

Taking selfies by the ruins

—Richard Reeve

Stamps of Dominion

Bridget Auchmuty

> *And he shall have dominion over the fish of the sea, and over the fowl of the air, and over the cattle, and over all the earth, and over every creeping thing that creepeth upon the earth* (GENESIS: I, 26)

My parents are finally shifting

We spend hours on triage
keep
        sell
                throw away
Twenty years of plastic bags
                        fabric scraps
                                wrapping paper
I'm a fine one to talk
                storing corks
                        tin cans
                                coils of wire

I have on board, my grandfather wrote,
several pets I got in Adelaide. A wallaby gave birth
soon after we left port. I thought it was a rat
until it climbed into its mother's pouch.

We divvy up the crested silver
not to take just yet
                but to record
expressions of interest
Unexpected—it's pitched me
into a kind of mourning

I have several animals and birds on board again
this homeward voyage, amongst them two opossums,
one of which got out and was found with its head
in the lime barrel and consequently died.

My old school friend is visiting from overseas
She loves her camera
                                        and her husband
is an amateur ornithologist

We collect the korimako
                                        riroriro
                                                    titipounamu
name them bellbird
                                        grey warbler
                                                    rifleman
tick off the boxes
                                        see a photograph in every landscape
frame and file
                                        record
                                                    preserve

Also a laughing jackass, a delightful
and most interesting bird but it died
early on the voyage. It was very tame
but I had no fresh meat to give it.

I'm throwing stones

We talk about the future—sideways
                                        when the time comes
                                                    eventually

Also monkeys, parrots and various birds.
I mean to add to the latter when we reach St Helena.
I've collected quite an aviary to take home:
twelve wax bills cost 2/-, and four canaries.

By the time they leave the trees are bare
                    oak
                                        poplar
                                                    sycamore

Recipe for a unitary state

Gail Ingram

Take those brown hills, lumpy
with glacial form, strewn with
ancient herb and kettle lake. Add
merino for a living, some rabbit
& stoats for sport. Let stoat prey
and rabbit proliferate.
Introduce calici, a beneficial
virus—sure to choke off
the excessive taste of rabbit.
By now the herbs will have reduced
to hieracium and dust. Pour in
a cow or two along with most
of the braided river. It will
reinvigorate the capital
gain. Don't mind the extra nutrients
in the run-off—what you lose
in black stilt, you'll gain in the creaming.

You'll know it's done when it has reached
a smooth grassy consistency
with no hint
of all that vexing tussock.

Water underground

Anthonie Tonnon

I'm still in awe
at how you pulled it all off
and driving through the drylands
seeing irrigators installed
I think about the coup
you turned the rules on themselves
you engineered that miracle
to free the water underground

they said you'd never take the council down
but you just found your way around

called it a national crisis
you were in bed with the press
you understood from experience how to
make it fast and hard to digest oh you
left them dumbfounded, unemployable
chose their replacements yourself
all their science from the cities couldn't keep you
from the water underground

they said you'd never take the council down
but you just found your way around
nine years out of power
you had time to think it out

she was one of those friends
followed the rabbit hole to its end
and you knew what it meant
to get involved

and the industry couldn't help you
no, none of the farmers who owed you
they let you fight in that pit alone

but with elections still on hold
with the cattle turning up by the truckload
you can hear the drills working now
on that water underground

Ghost stoat

Jonathan Cweorth

Winter lets you in
over barbs gentled by ice
past the wire's frozen pulse
you snowstep through the fence
unopposed

you elect yourself President for Life
in a secret ceremony
wearing a korowai of
pigeon feathers
fresh-plucked

you control it all
grip the dawn chorus by the throat
set the tūī gagging on loyalist anthems
dispatch a planeload of kiwi refugees
to seed other sanctuaries with fear

your enemies lay out poison buffets
soft beds lined with pheromone-laced straw
but you are past desire
a connoisseur only of power
and the purity of loneliness

in the cold vigilant nights,
you coin collective nouns:
a silence of mice
a nullity of rats
a void of possums

as you haunt your realm
a single lens records
your spotless coat
shining eyes
pawprints in the snow.

Super flumina Babylonis

Andrew Paul Wood

  Blue
tongue-flicking vipers bugloss, yellow
  pokers of mullein
    waving like Longinus' spear,
saffron orange
  California poppy *Eschscholzia* brought
on the boots of long-gone gold prospectors.

        Waimakariri
        Rakaia
        Waitaki
Three jade swords piercing the side
of a long Waitaha woman in a green mantle,
where in river-wombs somnambulant
  the eel ol' grey
    Papa Satan twists
    beneath white sky reflected from Antarctica.

Jezebel in the vineyard of Naboth, eh?
Send OCD Pilate some Sunlight soap,
he's got a lot of postcolonial dirt under his nails—
been there since his great, great granddaddy's time.

Water

Helen Watson White

For want of a few
nails the proclamation
was not raised

on a dry post in
a desert where
sheep once safely

roamed nibbling
green feed fattening
themselves for soup

and the dead left no
article of faith in the
future just excrement

and frozen soup they
died as it were leaving
no political will

Beach

Janet Newman

Some days the clouds disappear
on the drive to the coast

the way the things you wanted to say
evaporate when you get there.

Sentences float to the pencil-line horizon
between sky that is nothing but blue

and sea that is blue as …
but words fail you,

smudge like the fishing boats
in the distance without your binoculars

or the telescope mounted
in your absolutely beachfront window,

wash like driftwood
onto Kapiti's stony shore

where gulls patrol for intruders
to absolutely beachfront nesting grounds,

or drift to the Sounds
like discarded plastic

and wrap around mussel-farm ropes
or catch in cray pots,

loll beneath the surface
like snapper, gurnard and closer in

in warmer water, kahawai
swim out of reach,

or land on wet sand
netted, filleted, discarded.

Trawlers tear subjects from verbs,
drag contexts out to deeper water.

Soon the miles of driftwood on the beach
looks just like washed-up words,

the ones you wanted to use
pristine untrammelled calming

but found were of no use
although they seemed elegant

lying in your mind the way driftwood
shaped like big fish swimming reclines in gardens

but is truly uprooted trees
floated down the river, drained of colour,

pummelled until smooth
and left on the high water line to dry

just like the words you wanted to say,
jetsam on the tide.

waste management

Janet Charman

well this is awkward they've threatened to trespass me from the Carl's Junior Sandwich place over the road because i kept picking up the trash from their business which finds its way into the street and i've been leaving it outside their staff entrance

very irritating for them of course

today a staff member gripped my arm and said this is not our stuff we don't sell disposable nappies then when she said trespassed

i was dumbfounded all those petitions i sign for prisoners of conscience people rotting in jail for their beliefs

my terror knew no bounds so now i don't pick up the trash i just kick it from the kerb to the middle of the road

Story lines

Sue Fitchett

(A playful nod to erasure poet Mary Ruefle)

1.

pete takes us out to a tourist spot

pete's leg is falling apart
it's the glue

yet he drives us all
the way to Kaiteriteri

i point to those coastal mansions
mention rising sea

there's no climate change says pete
damn lies, a myth, hysteria

our car swerves round a corner
i sway in the back seat

next year pete's leg will be
reset with a stronger fix

if it starts tingling again in the future
the doctors will say *oh it's the glue*

pete believes in doctors
but scientists

that's another

2.
pete takes us out

pete's leg

drives us
to Kaiteriteri

rising sea

swerves round a corner

in the future

pete believes

3.
take us out

pete's falling apart

hysteria

in the back seat

tingling

another

4.

take out

those coastal mansions

sway

5.

akes

us

a myth

Old bones

John Howell

High tides seep into the garden. Again.
Too high. Too often.
The fence crumbles.

Bleached coral stalks the reef.

The Tuvalu Rev pours, at his sanctuary,
his stormy outburst to his ancestors.

The cyclone has wound the clock to breaking.
The graves are waterlogged canoes.
On higher ground he re-inters.
The benediction blown to the oceans.

Proposal for the Garden City

Doc Drumheller

Before the earthquakes crumbled our buildings
fields of orchards were bulldozed to build houses.

Now that they're gone, volunteer potatoes
self-seed abandoned back yards of the red zone.

Wild lettuce sows itself into vacant lots
parsley rises in between pavement cracks.

Empty carparks transform into greenhouses
for the homeless to sleep with tomatoes.

Watercress sprouts in construction-site streams
beans grow beside the river to fuel the rebuild.

The four avenues turn into an orchard
granny smith apples grow in the gutters.

Peel back the concrete to sow a new CBD
let the garden city reclaim its name.

Frankton Supermarket, Queenstown

Richard Reeve

for Tim

In Frankton supermarket, it is possible to buy a frozen Atlantic lobster.
Over for the day
                    from Hawea, past Cardrona, up the valley
to the pass where the road snails its way onto the Crown Range,
roll on up in your SUV, snowburnt, sunscreen-sweet, children

in the back, beer up the front, note foxgloves, fences, rabbits, the odd

poplars peering at real estate (never allowed in), mountain elbows
prodding each other for room. The subdivisions genuflect;
at Arrowtown we round up the boy in glib reminiscence,

eat a pizza called Glenorchy at one of the local pubs.
Taking selfies by the ruins, we are complex. Survivors,
we have become the presiding custodians of perspective,
paradisal grubs awaiting the gulp of a new long century.

By the fruit and veg, I sponsor the Remarkables with my eyes.
Eternal death, its blank face pressed up to the roof window,

browses today's specials, cold mountain ghosting a customer.

Dear ET

Harvey Molloy

The white dusting on our poles is melting.
Only bears and penguins live there.
Ice upon ice like a migraine in a stark neon-lit supermarket.
Ice like a sharp slap or a wake-up punch to the head.
Streams of melting snow fall down
shafts in the ice sheets,
which have their own name—*moulin*.

If you came when the plants grew the sky
or when the fish bloomed the sea
or when the lizards pounded forests,
come now to see the short-haired apes go apeshit.

Ends

Carolyn McCurdie

1.

I remember how he used to be funny,
that cartoon man on the street corner, wild-eyed
and lonely with his placard: *the end is nigh.*

Now here's the data. Here are the graphs.
Here are the aerial shots, the cracks
in the earth, in the ice.
Here are the first refugees.

Storm coming,
storm beyond our knowledge of storm.
Grief coming,
beyond our knowledge of grief.

2.

Slam the door. Pull the blinds.
Like a child, I dive to hide under the bed,
and find you there, already hiding.
You move, to make room.

You do this revolutionary thing—
you move to make room.

From your pocket you take out a square
of squashed chocolate.
Trade Aid, you say. You break it,
give one half to me.

You do this revolutionary thing—
give one half to me.

Warm melt in our mouths
as we talk about storm, grief,
our own jelly-livered weaknesses,
and yours, it turns out, are as bad as mine.

We do this revolutionary thing—
we tell the truth, we listen.

And you pull out your phone.

3.

Your phone—
a small crucible
that spills the world, its joy,
its stink, into your palm.

And I sink back to despair.
Because, there on your screen, the trolls,
the sad addicts of power and wealth,
who think they inhabit
some world that's not our world. Not Earth.

But, look. You scroll over continents,
islands, and the people, thousands of people
on beaches, in parks, in stone streets
hard with history. They're chanting.
They're singing, drumming, in oceans of banners,
placards held high: *the old story ends.*

What d'ya know, you say:
we are millions.

4.

We crawl out from under the bed,
crumpled, sticky. We have cobwebs
in our hair and we laugh
at how inspiring we're not.

We stand at the door, watch the wind
lift thistledown, sunlit, buoyant,
into the sky. Birds twitter on the roof.
Then we know—

song coming.
Song coming, beyond any
we've ever before lifted in song.

THE
REFUGEES ARE
CONFLICT
BEHIND EVERY
HUMAN SHIELD
GAZA
IRON DOME
WEANED EARLY FROM INNOCENCE
TO MATCH THE VIOLENCE IN WHICH WE LIVE
STING
IN THE AIR
WE ARE NOT SOFT THESE DAYS
GLOVES EVEN IN SUMMER

JOSTLING
IT WONT BE MUCH LONGER
PILLS BEFORE BED NOW
LOVE THE STRANGER AS YOURSELF
THERE IS NOTHING HERE FOR YOU
WILL THE WORLD
HOLD ON TO ME ANOTHER DAY
RED SEA FROM SUCH A HEIGHT
HOLDS HUNDREDS OF TERRORISTS

REPLACE WITH PROPHETS
THE NOISE IN THE DISTANCE IS NOT TOMORROW ANYMORE
GANGSTA
THIS POEM
CANNOT SAVE YOU
THOSE WERE OUR PEOPLE
TODAY
TŪ TIRA MAI NGĀ IWI
STITCH UP YOUR OWN MOUTH
LIKE ME OR YOU
BARBARIANS

DOGS OF EUROPE

[PART FOUR] CONFLICT

behind every human shield is another human shield

—Tusiata Avia

I cannot write a poem about Gaza

Tusiata Avia

for Izzeldin Abuelaish and everyone*

I cannot write a poem about Gaza because I cannot eat a whole desert.

I cannot write a poem about Gaza because I cannot go to bed with the stiff little babies and the bodies of children, there is no room for the little lost limbs, the disembodied arms yanked off like parts in a doll hospital.

I cannot write a poem about Gaza because if I speak up for the bodies of babies, for the pieces of children, for the women pulling out their own eyes, you will call me anti-Semitic and I must allow the blood of thousands to absolve me.

I cannot write a poem about Gaza because my fury and my grief will rise up out of my chest like a missile plotted on a computer in Tel Aviv, it will track me, pinpoint me and in a perfect arc, it will whine down out of the surgical sky, enter the top of my head and implode me.

I cannot write a poem about Gaza because Israel has a right to protect itself Israel has a right to protect itself Israel has a right to protect itself Israel has a right to protect itself Israel has a right to protect itself Israel has a right to protect itself Israel has a right to protect itself.

And Gaza does not.

I cannot write a poem about Gaza because behind every human shield is another human shield and another human shield and another human shield and another human shield and another human shield and another human shield. And behind that human shield—is a human.

---

* Izzeldin Abuelaish is a native of Gaza, a medical doctor, professor and the author of the book *I Shall Not Hate: A Gaza doctor's journey on the road to peace and human dignity*, which is, in part, about losing half of his family during an Israeli air strike. He is an important figure in Israeli/Palestinian relations and an avid advocate for young women. He founded Daughters for Life Foundation in memory of his three deceased daughters. He has recently been nominated for a Pulitzer Peace Prize.

I cannot write a poem about Gaza because it's complicated, so complicated, very, very complicated. So, I cannot write a poem about Gaza until I finish a PhD in Middle Eastern Politics and the Holocaust, until I am reborn a Jew and live under the Iron Dome* myself.

I cannot write a poem about Gaza because Tamar in Tel Aviv has got to get to the supermarket and the garden centre before the next siren. She's putting plants in their bomb shelter and the kids' favourite toys and treats, to make it less depressing.

I cannot write a poem about Gaza because Fatima in Gaza City has 58 seconds to evacuate her house with her babies before the missile strikes and the only way out is the sea. She has seen pictures on TV of babies thrown into pools and swimming instinctively.

I cannot write a poem about Gaza because there is an impenetrable iron dome that covers the entire state. It covers each mind and each heart, except for the few that line up and demand to be imprisoned.

I cannot write a poem about Gaza because of my friends: Tamar, Shira, Yael, Michal, Noya, David, Yair in Tel Aviv and Nazareth and Beersheva. Because every time I point to the blood-soaked I upset them, offend them, anger them, betray them. Let them go.

I cannot write a poem about Gaza because of my friend Izzeldin and his three exploded daughters and one exploded niece filleted across his living room.

I cannot write a poem about Gaza because I can do the maths. If two thousand one hundred and sixty-eight dead Palestinians divided by sixty-nine dead Israelis equals.† Find the true value of one Palestinian.

---

* The Iron Dome is a missile defence system developed by the Israeli Defence Forces.

† I wrote this poem at the beginning of August 2014; the numbers of dead were correct at the time but have since risen.

On the World News page

there's a photo of a nine-year-old boy
crouched at his father's feet
in a row of armed men wearing thawbs
and sandals, janbiya in their belts,
standing in the rubble of a war torn street,
the caption reads: *object of interest*

a rifle rests between his bony knees
butt balanced on the ground
barrel surrendered to the sky
callow hands reach to clasp the breech
as if it were a chalice
brimming with sweet milk

his curiosity a small shift
from reverence

a long shot from the stance of militia men
inured against wonder, well primed
to drink the bitter taste of blood

but he'll grow into it
this little hireling
weaned early from innocence
to take the lethal cup.

Elizabeth Brooke-Carr

On acquiring an Old Testament tone

Peter Bland

Words like 'barren'
and 'fruitful'
are beginning
to work their way
back. I warm
to their ancient weight
on my tongue. Perhaps
it's time for a ripe
Old Testament tone
to match the violence
in which we live?
Look around. Even
at a distance
have you ever seen
so much spilt blood,
so many innocents
dead in the streets,
so many crazed Samuels
Googling God?

Countdown

Mary Cresswell

When I open the window I smell spring in the air.
We can leap—or gambol—or spring in the air.

Let's pack up a picnic and take it outside.
Time to have our first fling in the air.

Diamonds in dewdrops, emeralds in leaves,
wherever we look there is bling in the air.

Over the mountains where birds never fly
a lazy volcano trails a string in the air.

In the canyons, shadows cut off at the pass:
both eagles and snakes fear the thing in the air.

The pack rats suffocate under the rocks
without enough daytime to bring in the air.

Sunset burns out as drones replace hawks—
nightfall takes over: the sting in the air.

How to train a paratrooper in 28 weeks

Elizabeth McRae

By the time a paratrooper passes out after 28 weeks' training he can:

1. With his bayonet, charge a sand-filled dummy on a gibbet and utter a prolonged howl.

2. Work a fibua—a Swedish-designed gizmo for fighting in built-up areas. (The army likes acronyms.)

3. Read at level three literacy—the level expected of a nine-year-old. (He came in at level one.)

He has completed his TAB—Tactical Advance to Battle. This is a 32-kilometre quick march carrying a 17-kilogram kit plus a rifle.

'We are not soft these days,' says the captain, 'and we have to be intelligent about it.'

He couldn't stand the sea

Marty Smith

That's how they learned to treat burns with saline
the ones in the sea healed better
but just when I'm really listening, she stops.

The men come in for smoko
just in the middle of
when she might have said *he lay on the fire.*

Gug's in his socks, woolly hat off
I'm in my flowered dress, leaning against him
seeing him out on the wing with blacksmoke curling off
the flames, the engine on fire, petrol pouring out,
still pouring over him.

He takes me down the tunnel of honeysuckle,
to the red wooden hayshed, sharp with straw
plays with his pups, passes one up.
I bury into its fat wrinkles
sniff up milk and soft, salt-smelling skin.

He stays home with the slow slouch of cows
wears a long-sleeved shirt and sometimes gloves
even in summer.

The plains of hesitation

Adrienne Jansen

On the plains of hesitation
a small crowd gathers.
They have their paintings and their pianos,
their china tea sets, their leather wallets.
They sit down on the grass uneasily,
their backs to the city, its streets bustling
with those who mind only their own business.

Far out on the edge of the plain
the refugees are jostling, hustling,
backpacks and water bottles, babies on hips,
maybe some bread, or maybe nothing.

The crowd on the plains of hesitation
look both ways, at the bustling city
and at the fleeing refugees.
Uncertainly they open their pianos,
play a sonata, drink some tea

while out on the other side of the city
the drums are beating, the guns are glinting
in the glaring sun, the flags are hoisted
and the troops are ready to charge.

On the Plains of Hesitation bleach the bones of countless millions who, at the Dawn of Victory, sat down to wait, and waiting—died!

—George W. Cecil (1891–1970)

The olives

Louise Wallace

She can't remember how she found out about the olives. Maybe it was from a travel piece in the glossy Sunday pullout. Or that TV programme where the chef goes to Europe, and *ooohs* and *aaahs* at things the locals have been doing for centuries, and where the food is all about *the simplicity*—fresh clams found with your feet, skirts held up above the waves, the clams gently sautéed over a driftwood fire then dressed with a white wine and parsley sauce, a hunk of fresh bread on the side to mop up. Or perhaps it was from one of those light, sunny movies where a middle-aged woman comes home to find her husband in bed with a young thing from the office, so she buys a decrepit house in Italy which she spends the summer renovating, and she grows on the townspeople who she hires to help with the renovations but who also teach her about herself. Men watch the newly single woman dancing in a bar from the dimly lit entrance and they smile at her youthful exuberance—surprising for her age. There was something about a man with a large moustache, a donkey and an emergency as well, but mostly she remembers the olives, and the way they were collected. Tarpaulins were laid under the trees and you had to shake the life out of the branches. She remembers the sound of the olives falling onto the tarp, like rain on the roof from the inside of a car. When people are shooting other people for having a good time/ When people voice heartbreak for those who were shot and are then criticised by yet other people, because there's heartbreak happening in many other places as well and they should feel heartbreak for those people too—equal-opportunity heartbreak—which is true, but she doesn't think they're bad people, they just watch the six o'clock news/ When she wonders how much more heartbreak we can actually all carry before our shoulders give way, before they buckle and crack under all this heartbreak/ Then that is what she wants to hear—the sound of olives falling onto a tarp, bouncing, then settling, *pat pat pat*. That is the sound she would like to go to sleep by. She would like to buy an app for that. She would like the last thing she hears coming from her phone at night to be the *pat pat pat* of a shower of olives, a storm of them, room for nothing else outside. But there *is* no app for that and there are no dreams to fall asleep for, there is only now, and the only *pat pat pat* is the sound of the rain hitting the back of her neck and the neck of her father and the small necks of her two young daughters, curled over in the boat, their heads bowed like plants weighed down by water, rain soaking their hair, their hair's ends dangling by their ankles, dripping into the puddle their feet are steeping in. She doesn't look up at the size of the waves. She spends the long dark hours talking to her daughters, saying the same things over and over to soothe them, to drown out the sound of the water sloshing against the sides of the boat—*don't look back/ it will be okay/ it won't be much longer/ I'm here/ we are together/ hold tight/ hold on to one another/ don't cry/ don't scream.*

We're all exiles, Kevin says

Mercedes Webb-Pullman

Early this summer refugees began to appear at our beach. Kevin says you can tell refugees by their birthmarks which are not like ours. They also have six toes.

They walk around our village in pairs or small groups in clouds of strange languages. They stare at our houses and hills full of trees as if they recognise them, though they've never been here before. They often go inside our church where children who peer through windows say they take pictures of each other behind the altar where only priests should be.

When they first appeared we had a plague of seven-spotted ladybirds, which are a sign of welcome. Except smaller and darker like inside an old curled photo. We have to take pills before bed now. Kevin says our duty is to save things. Kevin says they've come too late.

Calais haiku

Sarah Paterson

Cycle 1: Us

Every day here
we say will be the last one.
Maybe tomorrow.

Stones roll past Sarwan's
tent flap. His eyes bear the pain
of 12,000 more.

Rommel sits alone.
He is never alone, he
is always alone

Zimarko carries
supplies to the school he builds
though he has no house

Mahmoud gives to me
his last remaining sugar
from his best glass jar.

Cycle 2: Mud

A single glove lies
beneath fresh mud. A hand
outstretched towards you

New rain makes fresh hell,
fresh wind brings newcomers
and blankets are scarce

A dim light flashes
from the Afghan club tonight—
ports in lonely storms

Cycle 3: Walls

If the doors stay closed
my family will die here.
The walls are weapons.

Inshallah in U
K, Inshallah we'll meet on
Earth, as in heaven.

I hope that the dirt
on my feet, my hands, my hair
never leaves my mind.

Tampons can light fires
wet hair can wash hands clean
I can make you smile.

If love were passports
this place would vanish forever
under its own weight.

Cycle 4: Bible

This God commands you,
love the stranger as yourself,
for you too once fled.

You gave me a drink,
you sheltered and fed angels
thinking they were men.

God is my refuge,
for in the lands of the earth
here I have found none.

Dark water

Victor Billot

There is nothing here for you.
There is no light above the door that says that home is near.
You will not cast your arms around your father's neck
and rest your head in the bedroom's evening quiet.

There is nothing here for you.
There is no laughter nor a mother's lips to calm your tears.
You will not see the summer clouds of the land they sought,
but breathe the smell of fear and diesel fumes upon the night.

There is nothing here for you.
There are no voices from the kitchen talking gently as you sleep.
You will not learn new songs or squabble with your brother now.
Dark water draws the warmth from life.
Dark water fills our hearts.

Displaced

Majella Cullinane

He walked like that west and west and north.
Until at nightfall under freezing stars they arrived …

—'Quarantine', EAVAN BOLAND

Hear the ghosts panning gold at sunset,
their calls and laughter snagging the gravel earth;
beneath a juniper sky the flap of tarpaulin,
a canvas door slowly opening.

Forward one hundred years, a woman emerging:
a glimpse of dark hair, a white head scarf,
her golden bracelets glistening,
can you hear her voice asking—
will the world hold on to me another day?

How far she has walked, her feet mapping
all those who have come before her. Remember,
your ancestors who slept on hard soil,
moss and charlock for bedding
their dreams spilling into their shivering breaths,
dreams attuned to the road's long black song.

We are far from what we know:
here, the kererū winnowing the cold air,
a whistle signalling the end of a rugby game,
lonely boy-racers skidding past midnight.
If the stars could burn into our smallness,
our breathing, slide under the fractures
of our loss, our unbelonging,
what would they answer her?

The view from the space shuttle

Jane Graham George

Looking at the Red Sea from such a height, John Glenn remarked on its beauty and wished mankind could settle its differences in that troubled region. But imagine if the shuttle came loose from its invisible moorings, lost radio contact with Houston, and supplies of food and water began to run low. The astronauts might squabble fiercely over the last chocolate bar, the Red Sea might become the emblem of man's nature, spill over across the continents and other swelling seas, and dim the twinkling lights of Wellington. Facing hunger and discord, would John Glenn calm the young crew, remind them to look at the supple curve of the Earth, blanketed with soft cloud like floating milkweed or dandelion seed? Could the astronauts meditate on the oceans blue as an indigo bunting, blue as Aphrodite's heaven, blue as the chant that rises and escapes the Gothic spire to fill this and all the bright galaxies?

United Nations International Day of Peace 2013

A people's guide to disarmament

Catherine Amey

There are flower bombs
and seed bombs
and Food Not Bombs
stockpiled outside the weapons fair
Some sleepy peace activists
are dishing out dumpstered pumpkin soup
with tea and scones for afters
infusing the morning air
with breakfast
not war
I pull a panda suit over my jeans
and enfold surprised joggers
in fluffy hugs
these fragile stranger caresses
are all the arms we need

The delegates are whisked in through the back door
so we cannot scream at them
or embrace them
or offer them soup
They are not all grey businessmen
some are young and female
some are queer or disabled
this is an equal-opportunities way of killing
celebrating diversity among the dealers
if not the dead
I wonder, do they play with their children
water pistols spraying in the sunlight
until everyone is dripping with laughter
do they sing hymns on Sunday
do they say their prayers
to the Maker of Mines?

All the flower bombs
fall to pieces
but not into peace
The teenage pacifists
pour paper cups of soup
and watch it spilt on the ground
The seed bombs are scattered
but have yet to germinate

Still it takes just ten minutes
to disarm the delegates
One call to the police
fully justified
for this well-mannered conference
holds hundreds of terrorists
and lethal weapons inside

Global

Emma Neale

Search for counter-attack
Replace with hold
Search for attack
Replace with attach
Search for murdered
Replace with heard
Search for killed
Replace with serenaded
Search for ambushed
Replace with invited
Search for missile launchers
Replace with oh, red silk fans
Search for front line
Replace with lamp-lit threshold
Search for grenades
Replace with iris bulbs
Search for smart bombs
Replace with crayoned paper folded into lilies, swans
Search for generals
Replace with farmers, orchardists, gardeners, mechanics, doctors,
    veterinarians, school teachers, artists, painters, housekeepers, marine
    biologists, zoologists, nurses, musicians
Search for combatants
Replace with counsellors, conductors, bus drivers, ecologists, train drivers,
    sailors, firefighters, ambulance drivers, historians, solar engineers,
    designers, seamstresses, artesian well-drillers, builders
Search for profits
Replace with prophets
Save as
New World.doc

Dear Messrs Smith & Wesson

James Norcliffe

I have located you and your dream
in my shoulder holster.
Do you mind if I join you?

Do you mind if I draw you
with your sideburns just a little
singed and powder-burnt?

Somehow the dream has shifted
from the dusty main street,
the verandas and hitching posts

to asphalt freeways, to black SUVs.
The rain has turned to hail,
sunshine to sodium and neon.

I was a stakeholder in your dream,
dear Smith, dear Wesson, but
you've made my stake obsolete,

though I guess it was ever useless,
never fitting in the glovebox, having
no heft in the cradle of my hand.

You must know that heroes have gone
the way of horses, and the noise
in the distance is not tomorrow any more.

Gangsta as

Michael Botur

Gangsta as Sky City's high-rollin clan-lab Chinese
Gangsta as Premo Block D. Gangsta as the Sindi.
Gangsta as the Blenheim iwi-Lone Legion beef

Gangsta as Celtics singlets bandagin bleedin Bloods
Gangsta as craniums cracked on kerbs by kinghittin thugs
Gangsta as a Nelson league team givin gooks the bum's rush

Gangsta as sandpaper scalps and swastika-stickered skin
Gangsta as the hoodrats Becroft's too soft to discipline,
and that nerd's arm snappin, and the Harris Gang chucklin.

Gangsta as the Hudsons, the Duffys, the Browns
Gangsta as the Fourth Reich guy with *Die Nigger Die* tatted on his brow
Gangsta as the Police Gang on the prowl.

Gangsta as the freedom to associate.
Gangsta as the Killer Clown Fiends' prison Ritalin trade
Gangsta as solitary Gs catchin up on their lost NCEA

Gangsta as that black and spewin Bay of Plenty pollutant: the Filthy Few
Gangsta as the Nomads, Horowhenua's rotten tooth
Gangsta as Mossie's tangi, the thousand-long lunchline queue.

Gangsta as a dozen Road Knights beside you at the Timaru traffic lights.
Gangsta as the *Snitches Get Stitches* patches Angels let you buy online
Gangsta as the stubborn Tribesmen on their Jap bikes

Gangsta as Junior Warriors gettin jumped on the Viaduct
Gangsta as the Wairoa Mob's scrum for top dog
Gangsta as shot mobsters refusin to see a doctor.

Gangsta as staunchin out a teacher.
Gangsta as havin a different dad every month
And every afternoon, when she wakes up, you get a few crumbs of mum.

Protection order

Nicola Thorstensen

This poem cannot deflect a bullet.
It will not stop a fist or a boot.
It can't issue a proximity alert.

This poem is not a panic button,
a security detail,
or a rapid response team.

It won't deadbolt the window,
sheath the knife,
dull the blade.

It won't facilitate time
travel so you can un-meet that stranger.
It can't be your guardian angel.

It is neither Kevlar suit nor Mithril vest.
It's not even a nosy neighbour
speed-dialling 111 behind the blinds.

It will not force your assailant to face down
a phalanx of vigilantes.
It will not morph jagged glass to sugar.

This poem can not save you.

Reportage

Michael Steven

The fractured towns associate

—W.H. Auden

1

Friends of the departed have gathered
on a mild Sunday morning, early in May.
In gold: a name, two dates; lines of pertinent scripture
emblazoned across the marble headstone.

They said it was the war to rewrite the law.
At either end of Stafford Street: roadblocks,
armed police, the black menace of their M-16s.
The government said it was the last straw.

No one saw the trouble in the town escalate.
No one paid attention to small scuffles
taking place each day outside the courthouse.
It wasn't unusual. It was what bikers did.

2

During roll call at the periodic detention centre
the day's detainees stand about, gossiping;
cadging smokes; awaiting assignment to work gangs.
The warden is trained to notice signs of tension.

During roll call at the periodic detention centre,
the first victim takes a blade in his jugular.
No one sees a thing. No one will name the hitter.
The warden is trained to administer CPR.

At a clandestine location: a clandestine meeting.
There is talk of losing face, of the need for swift reprisal.

Roles are assigned. Firearms are stealthily distributed.
The warden is seconds too late administering CPR.

3

From the main centres, journalists converge.
The daily broadsheets ink tabloid copy;
the 'Riviera of the South' becomes a media hotspot.
Parliament appoints a new Hooverian gangbuster.

A current events show sends skilled cameramen.
Their apertures open on bearded men wearing leathers
drinking in garden bars; on rows of polished motorcycles;
on compounds fortified with roofing iron, razor wire.

The town quickly assumes an under-siege mentality.
En route from points north and points south,
travellers make comparisons with Belfast.
The town waits for things that go bang at night.

4

Windows boarded over with sheets of plywood.
Residents take to their homes before dark.
A cul-de-sac is peppered with rounds, spent shell casings.
A parcel of Semtex pancakes a trucking yard.

The gangbuster delivers heated sermons to his caucus.
Funding is allocated. A taskforce is established.
The taskforce taps phones, gathers data from paid informants.
They bust down doors; use tear gas to make arrests.

The acclaimed photographer adjusts her lens.
The grieving friends bow their heads.
Over the mulch of the newly tilled plot,
they are pouring libations from brown bottles.

No time like the 80s

Airini Beautrais

In 1989, my dad gets knocked off his motorbike.
He gets a court summons to testify against the driver.
Because she is brown, and my dad has decided
the justice system is racist, he rips up the summons.

A few weeks earlier, a housebreaker (brown)
who happened to be a father of six
was shot dead by a neighbour (white)
who was let off.

Dad rips up his summons on the *Holmes* show.
It is very exciting. Reporters come to our house.
I put on my best hair-tie, the one with a gauze flower,
and my siblings and I roll around the floor on camera.

After it screens, the phone calls start.
'I'm going to drop a bomb on your house,'
a weirdo tells my mother.
And another weirdo, or possibly the same one

is going to rape, torture and murder
my sister and me (four and six).
Like Holmes used to say,
those were our people today.

It is the end of a dark decade. One that began
with: Sport and politics shouldn't mix,
with the Red Squad, chanting:
Root more, eat more, drink more piss.

Ronald Reagan was thinking neutron. It was illegal
for men to make love to each other. American warships
were being officially welcomed into our harbours
and unofficially welcomed by rabble-rousers,

my parents included, paddling out in kayak
and mullet boat. They lived their lives
as though there wasn't a madman on the trigger
although there was—in fact, there were several.

The Russians flying jets into British airspace,
and the British flying theirs in circles around them,
like some bizarre avian courtship, a dance of death.
'You'd seen films about Hiroshima,' my dad says,

'100,000 people being incinerated.' Did you think
nuclear war was a definite possibility? 'Oh, shit yes.
And you'd ask yourself, what would you do, if they bombed Auckland?
Would you run away, or run towards it?'

What went through Reagan's head, as he shifted
from butt cheek to butt cheek? Or Thatcher's? Brezhnev's?
We'll never know. My mother hangs up the phone.
My father stops riding a motorbike. They live their lives.

We aren't allowed water pistols. They give us balloons
that read 'I want to grow up not blow up'.
We sew a patchwork peace flag:
Tūtira mai ngā iwi.

In 1990, on Hiroshima Day, we dig a hole in the sand,
put a kauri tree in. We throw some flowers,
like there aren't new wars unfolding,
although there are.

The heart jumps up in fear to see the mouths

Bernadette Hall

St Mary of the Angels, Rome

There are Polish sculptures on the bronze doors, two young
men, their heads bandaged, their mouths also covered with cloth.
Inside, there's the huge Carrera marble head of John the Baptist,
his mouth with tapes across it. The heart jumps up in fear
to see the mouths bandaged up like this, the cloth tied so tightly.

The angel flies out of the wall. She bends before him.
She marvels at the mechanical contraption of his wings. Maybe
she goes down on one knee. The curve of her back
is like the sweet curve of a hill, a hill with water running steady
through its deep roots, a hill that's holy in its green silence.

What does it take to cut out the tongue of another?
What does it take to stitch up your own mouth? To not say
as some of them refuse to say? And then it's left up to those others
to make the body do the talking. What does it take to do nothing?

She will do something. And we will be left to pray,
just as we prayed for the horses at Borodino.

The wall: a love story, of sorts

Michelle Elvy

You remember our first dance? You there, me here: a mismatched pair. You held out your hand. I didn't know you, but you pulled me up, up, up … and I let go of everything and found myself in the arms of a strangely familiar stranger. We were high, floating on a wild November night. Hot breath, cold sweat, embracing an orgy of frenzy, noise, delight. We marvelled at the night, argued about wrong and right. I drank your Coke, you smoked my F6. Just like a commercial.

Three years later and we're *making* commercials, only this time it's Vita-Cola-Realpolitik and you keep saying *baby, we're selling what sells.* You and me and Ostalgie. Don't worry that the kid's crying; Mama and Papa are self-employed. *Achtung, baby,* you keep saying, like it means something. But you still haven't learnt my language.

And now we don't fight about wrong and right but the bottom fucking line and the Turks living upstairs and the bicycles crowding the entryway of our apartment building. *I need to get in and out,* you say. I'm sick of the Marlboro Man but I pull long and hard anyway and can't help but laugh when you come to bed wearing a stiff shit-green Vopo hat you call a relic, a *find.* Still, I feel a worry growing in my gut, wonder if our children will be more like *me* or *you*, and I realise what I really mean is whether they'll be more like *us* or *them.*

Barbarians have crossed at the border

Pat White

Remembering Cavafy

When the barbarians do come, they will not
wear jackboots or have polished epaulettes
their uniforms, no clue to who they might be
you will know them only when they want
your thoughts and ask you to leave them
at the doorstep like the milk bottles. Do it
do anything at all.
                    When the barbarians arrive
and they start singing familiar songs of love
and longing for home, don't be surprised, be
prepared to steal their chickens and ring
their necks.
            Because, you will know them
when they ask where your daughter is
and you have to tell them she's run to
the mountains where she steals favours
in return for forbidden fruit. She warned
the barbarians would arrive, causing heroes
to appear on television, and old women to scavenge
in garbage or young men to kill their own meat
while old men will gather at the pub to talk about
better days, always other days. They are not
to be relied on to do a thing, anything at all.

Do you wish to survive while the barbarians
window-shop in your neighbourhood? Do not
read their poster of friendly intentions, lie
blatantly, even with your hand on your heart
blaspheme kneeling in front of the altar; betray
your mother with a glance, look on when your
uncle is taken away without question; learn to

steal just enough, cheat your neighbour, trust
only your own judgement, and blame, always
blame the barbarians, for their good intentions,
money to spend, lovers at home, their civil ways
phony olive branches, release of flightless doves
their words in many tongues.

Oh yes, when

the barbarians walk your streets
and the scent of them is in the air you breathe
we rely on you to do anything, anything at all
anything it takes.

Prague 2013: the heart of Europe

Paul Schimmel

This narrow circle encompasses my entire life.

—Franz Kafka

Each end foreshadowed
in its beginning. Whatever
passed, or failed to pass,
from baby to mother; back
from mother to baby, a life's
sentence was delivered
here: U Radnice 5, Prague
Old Town, July 3rd, 1883.

Franz Kafka will spend
his days circling the void,
in darkness tracing cracks
within the castle walls, re-
living his trial; deferring
with words, his fate:
to die 'like a dog'.

In cities of art and artifice,
the violence is gone under-
ground; limbs severed,
bodies shattered by sword,
graves without name and
numberless. Without empire
to conquer now, the dingy
rabble of anarchists, neo-
Nazis, ruthless technocrats,
all manner of mindless
thugs, patrol the perimeters.
The dogs of Europe are mostly
silent; muzzled and waiting.

Beacon fire

Carolyn McCurdie

An image has snagged itself in my mind.
It is making demands of me.

A night sky. Stars. Against these
the dark presence of the hill
you and I have known all our lives.
From early morning we've been carrying wood
to the top. And all day, as we picked splinters
from our palms, we have watched
another hill along the coast where the land curves
into the unknown.

Is this memory? A fragment of ancestor
still in the blood?

Then, just as we think about sleep
that hill flings fire to the sky
and there's shouting. We have prepared
the torch. Our own beacon fire stutters
then opens its throat. For a moment
we stare at our hill. We have never seen it
so urgent. A repeating,
repeating of hills, but we're too busy to look.
Children, still curled with sleep
are blanket-bundled into carts to send them away
from the coast. Most of the food goes with them.

Is it something I've read? A novel? A history?

We are left, the grown-ups. We pace, we sharpen,
we wait. Then the moment we stand, walk out
to face the thunderous oncoming.

I'm aware of your shoulder.
I hear your attempt to calm
your breathing. I try to calm mine
and fail. But there are so many of us, so many of us.

Or could this be from the future?
There will be a child. One of ours.
Her voice swept back by storm,
by rising tide, does she use mind,
splinter, fire, to cry out?

ABOUT THE CONTRIBUTORS

Johanna Aitchison was the New Zealand participant in the University of Iowa's International Writing Program in 2015. Her latest volume of poetry, *Miss Dust*, was described by Sarah Quigley as 'Emily Dickinson for the 21st century'. She lives in Palmerston North and runs, snowboards and lifts weights in her spare time.

Ivy Alvarez is the author of *The Everyday English Dictionary* (Paekakariki Press, 2016), *Hollywood Starlet* (dancing girl press, 2015), *Disturbance* (Seren, 2013) and *Mortal* (Red Morning Press, 2006). Born in the Philippines and raised in Australia, she lived almost 10 years in Wales before moving to New Zealand in 2014. See ivyalvarez.com

Catherine Amey is a librarian, writer and baker from Wellington. The peace and animal rights movements are close to her heart, and she believes that collectively we can create a better world. She lives with the love of her life in a tiny house with a wild garden by the sea.

Nick Ascroft is a nihilist from North Otago. He is also a non-fiction author writing on sport, music and punctuation. He lives in Wellington. 'Procyclical' is included in his most recent collection of poetry, *Back with the Human Condition* (VUP, 2016).

Bridget Auchmuty lives in rural Nelson and has a Master's of Creative Writing from Massey University. Her fiction and poetry have been published in various anthologies and journals including *JAAM*, *Meniscus* and *Mslexia*.

Tusiata Avia is a Samoan-New Zealand poet, performer and writer. Her third collection of poetry, *Fale Aitu/Spirit House* (VUP, 2016), which was long-listed in the 2017 Ockham New Zealand Book Awards, includes 'I cannot write a poem about Gaza'. Tusiata has held a number of writers' residencies and awards. She teaches creative writing and performing arts at Manukau Institute of Technology.

Serie Barford was born in Aotearoa to a migrant German-Samoan mother and a Palagi father. Her latest collection, *Entangled Islands* (Anahera Press, 2015), combines poetry with prose. Her work has appeared in multidisciplinary books, journals and websites. Some of Serie's short stories have been adapted for radio.

Nell Barnard is a poet and priest living in Auckland. She holds an MA (Writing) from Iowa, and studied at Duke and Otago. 'Cabin fever' was inspired by her own experience and her work with women in refuge. On behalf of these sisters, she is pleased to be included in this project.

Airini Beautrais lives in Whanganui. She is the author of three collections of poetry, most recently *Dear Neil Roberts* (VUP, 2014), which includes 'No time like the 80s'. Airini won the Landfall Essay Competition 2016.

Victor Billot is a Dunedin writer who has published two books of poetry: *Mad Skillz for the Demon Operators* (2014) and *Machine Language* (2015), which includes 'Dark water'. An album of his poetry set to music is currently being produced by the group Alpha Plan. See www.victorbillot.com

Peter Bland's latest collection, *A Fugitive Presence* (Steele Roberts, 2016) includes his poem 'On acquiring an Old Testament tone'. He is currently working on a new book of poems for children, and collecting material for the second part of his memoirs.

Michael Botur of Whangarei has published creative writing in *Landfall, Poetry New Zealand, JAAM, Takahe, Bravado, Catalyst* and a bunch of journals no one cares about. He is author of three short story collections and has published journalism in the likes of the *NZ Herald, Sunday Star-Times* and *Mana*. 'Gangsta as' was first published in *Takahē 78*.

Elizabeth Brooke-Carr lives and writes in Dunedin. From her hillside eyrie the contours of the city hills and harbour, shoreline and horizon enlarge her vision; the diversity of life in and beyond feeds her imagination. Her writing often explores social justice issues.

Diane Brown runs Creative Writing Dunedin and is the author of seven books, including *Learning to Lie Together* (Godwit Press, 2004), *Eight Stages of Grace* (Vintage, 2002), *Here Comes Another Vital Moment* (Godwit Press, 2006) and *Taking My Mother to the Opera* (OUP, 2015).

Nigel Brown is a well-known New Zealand painter. He has had a long association with poets including R.F. Brown, Riemke Ensing and Glenn Colquhoun. Text, often his own, features in much of his work. His poetry has previously appeared in *The Vernacularist* (The Depot, Auckland) and recently his paintings featured in publications *Eborakon* and *Cordite*. He lives in Dunedin.

Janet Charman is an award-winning Auckland poet whose current practice engages with the Matrixial theory of human connectivity as located in the feminine (as advanced in the writings of Bracha Ettinger).

Mary Cresswell is from Los Angeles and lives on the Kāpiti Coast. *Fish Stories*, her collection of environmental poems in ghazal and other forms, was published by Canterbury University Press in 2015.

Majella Cullinane writes poetry and fiction. She was Robert Burns Fellow in 2014, and is currently studying for a PhD in creative practice at the Centre for Irish & Scottish Studies at the University of Otago. She lives in Port Chalmers with her partner Andrew and their son Robbie.

Jonathan Cweorth is a Dunedin poet and playwright. His poems have been published in journals in New Zealand and overseas, and a number of his scripts for puppet plays, masques, fire dances and aerial silks performances have featured in local arts festivals. He enjoys working in writing groups.

Alison Denham has had work appear in poetry journals and anthologies in New Zealand, the UK and the US. In 2014 her second collection of poems, *Raspberry Money*, was published by Sudden Valley Press. She lives and works in Dunedin as a business analyst.

Doc Drumheller has worked in award-winning theatre and music groups and has published 10 collections of poetry. His poems have been translated into more than 20 languages, and he has performed widely overseas and throughout New Zealand. He lives in Oxford, where he edits and publishes the literary journal *Catalyst*.

Nicola Easthope is an English and psychology teacher at Kāpiti College. Her first collection of poetry, *leaving my arms free to fly around you*, was published by Steele Roberts in 2011. She is currently writing her second collection, *Working the Tang*. She was a guest poet at the Queensland Poetry Festival in 2012.

Lynley Edmeades' poetry, reviews and scholarship have been published in New Zealand, the US, Europe and Australia. Her debut poetry collection, *As the Verb Tenses* (OUP, 2016), was long-listed in the 2017 Ockham New Zealand Book Awards. She has just completed a doctoral thesis at the University of Otago on sound in avant-garde poetics.

Murray Edmond is the author of 14 books of poetry and editor of three poetry anthologies and the critical journal *Ka Mate Ka Ora*. His recent publications include *Then It Was Now Again: Selected critical writing* (Atuanui Press, 2014); *Shaggy Magpie Songs* (AUP, 2015) and *Strait Men and Other Tales* (Steele Roberts, 2015).

David Eggleton lives in Dunedin where he is the editor of *Landfall* and Landfall Review Online. He has published seven books of poems as well as a number of books of fiction and non-fiction. In 2016 David's *The Conch Trumpet* won the

Ockham New Zealand Award for Poetry, and later in the year he received the Prime Minister's Award for Literary Achievement in Poetry.

Chris Else is a novelist and reviewer who lives in Dunedin. He spent two years teaching English at the Albanian State University, Tirana, in the 1970s. Currently, alongside his wife, Barbara Else, he runs a literary agency and manuscript assessment service.

Michelle Elvy is a writer, editor and manuscript assessor, based in the Bay of Islands, but currently sailing in East Africa aboard her sailboat, *Momo*. She edits at *Flash Frontier* (where 'The wall' first appeared) and *Blue Five Notebook* and is assistant editor for the critically acclaimed *Best Small Fictions* series. See michelleelvy.com & svmomo.blogspot.com

Jessie Fenton entered her first poetry slam by accident, and hasn't been able to stop since. She came second in the 2015 New Zealand Poetry Slam and went on to win Poetry Idol at the 2016 Auckland Writers' Festival. These days she writes most of her poems while on her bike to law school.

Sue Fitchett is a Waiheke Islander, conservationist and long-term political activist. She is also co-author or editor of several poetry books including *Palaver Lava Queen* (AUP, 2004) and *On the Wing* (Steele Roberts, 2014). Her work has appeared in various publications in New Zealand and Australia and at art shows.

Janis Freegard's most recent publications are a novel *The Year of Falling* (Mākaro Press, 2015) and a poetry collection *The Glass Rooster* (AUP, 2015), in which 'Arohata' appears. Born in the UK, she grew up in South Africa, Australia and New Zealand. She lives in Wellington and works in the state sector.

Kathleen Gallagher received the New Zealand Playwrights Award in 1993. She has written 16 plays for professional theatre and radio, and three collections of poetry, and produced and directed six feature films. In 2004 she received the Sonja Davies Peace Award for the film *Tau Te Mauri Breath of Peace*. Her first novel, *Earthquakes and Butterflies*, was abridged on RNZ National in February 2016.

Rhian Gallagher's first poetry collection, *Salt Water Creek* (Enitharmon Press, 2003) was shortlisted for the Forward Prize for First Collection. She received the Janet Frame Literary Trust Award in 2008. Her second collection, *Shift* (AUP, 2011; Enitharmon Press, 2012) won the New Zealand Post Book Award for Poetry in 2012.

Jane Graham George was born in the US. Her books—*Aotearoa: New Zealand poems*, *Library Land* and *A Year on the Kāpiti Line & Other Poems* (which includes 'The view from the space shuttle')—were published by Red Dragonfly Press. She has lived in California and Minnesota and currently lives on the Kāpiti Coast, where she works as a librarian.

Anahera Gildea (Ngāti Raukawa-ki-te-Tonga, Ngāi-te-Rangi, Ngāti Toa Rangatira, Te Āti Awa, Kāi Tahu) is a writer and 'artivist'. Her first book, *Poroporoākī: Weaving the Via Dolorosa*, was published by Seraph Press in 2016. She holds a BA in art theory, graduate diplomas in psychology, teaching and performing arts, and a Master's degree in creative writing from Victoria University.

Paula Green is a poet, reviewer, anthologist and children's author with a doctorate in Italian. She has published ten poetry collections including three for children. Co-written with Harry Ricketts, her book *99 Ways into New Zealand Poetry* was shortlisted for the New Zealand Book Awards. She runs the blog New Zealand Poetry Shelf. Her poem 'First impressions' was published in *The Baker's Thumbprint* (Seraph Press, 2013).

Bernadette Hall lives in a renovated bach at Amberley Beach in the Hurunui, North Canterbury. Poetry has taken her to Iowa, Ireland and Antarctica. She has published 10 collections, her most recent being *Life & Customs* (VUP, 2013), which includes her poem 'The heart jumps in fear to see the mouths', and *Maukatere, floating mountain* (Seraph Press, 2016). In 2015 she received the Prime Minister's Award for Literary Achievement in Poetry.

Sandi Hall is an award-winning novelist whose books include *The Godmothers* (Women's Press, 1982), *Wingwomen of Hera* (Spinsters Ink, 1987) and *Rumours of Dreams* (Spinifex, 2003). Mercury Theatre staged her first play, *Change of Heart*, and TVNZ screened *Just Passing Through*, her future-fiction drama. She has won two poetry slams. All her work has a feminist focus. In her poem the references for Meri Te Tai's speech and translation are: Angela Ballara, 'Mangakahia, Meri Te Tai': www.teara.govt.nz/en/biographies/2m30/mangakahia-meri-te-tai; and Bridget Williams et al. (eds), *The Book of New Zealand Women*, Bridget Williams Books, 1991.

Ruth Hanover's writing has been shaped by a degree in English, ESOL teaching in Cairo and Stockholm, a duty of care for family (Alzheimer's), travel, and being in therapy. Ruth has written a first novel (unpublished), short fiction, and poetry. She has had work published in *Takahē* and also anthologised. Two of her poems were placed (third and commended) in the New Zealand Poetry Society's International Poetry Competition 2016, and her work has recently appeared in *London Grip*.

Michael Harlow is the author of 10 books of poetry. He has held numerous fellowships and residencies, and has been awarded the Lauris Edmond Memorial Award for Distinguished Contribution to Poetry. *Nothing for it but to Sing* won the

Kathleen Grattan Award Poetry in 2015, and was published by Otago University Press in 2016. His poem 'Bite the coin its brilliance' appears in that collection.

Siobhan Harvey is the author of five books, including the 2013 Kathleen Grattan Poetry Award winner *Cloudboy* (Otago University Press, 2014). She co-edited *Essential New Zealand Poems* (Godwit, 2014). She is a lecturer at the Centre for Creative Writing at AUT, and was runner-up in the 2015 and 2014 New Zealand Poetry Society International Poetry competitions. Her poem 'Serving notice upon the prime minister' appeared first in *Poetry New Zealand 50* (2015).

Trevor Hayes lives and works in Punakaiki. He has had poems published in *JAAM*, *Sport*, *Landfall*, *Poetry New Zealand* and *Takahē*.

Jeffrey Paparoa Holman writes poetry, memoir and history. His most recent works are *The Lost Pilot: A memoir* (Penguin, 2013) and *Shaken Down 6.3* (poetry, Canterbury University Press, 2012). New poetry titles *Blood Ties* (New and Selected, CUP) and *Dylan Junkie* (Mākaro Press) are due early in 2017.

David Howard spent 35 years writing *The Incomplete Poems* (Cold Hub Press, 2011). He edited *A Place to Go On From: The collected poems of Iain Lonie* (OUP, 2015). 'A display case in the Museum of Communism' was composed while he held a Unesco City of Literature Residency in Prague (2016).

John Howell lives in Ngaio, Wellington. Recently he retired from ministering at the Union Parish in Taupo. His current interests are poetry, and the ethics of climate change. He has published two books of prayers. He volunteers one day a week with the homeless.

Gail Ingram's poetry and short stories have been published in New Zealand and overseas. She was a finalist for 2016 Best Small Fictions, and won the 2016 international New Zealand Poetry Society competition. She has recently completed a poetry collection for her Master's at Massey University.

Kevin Ireland lives in Devonport. His *Selected Poems* appeared in 2013, followed by two further collections, *Feeding the Birds* in 2014 (which includes 'A song for happy voters'), and *Looking Out to Sea* in 2015 (all Steele Roberts). His 23rd book of poems, *Humphrey Bogart's Great Sacrifice*, was recently published, also by Steele Roberts, Wellington.

Adrienne Jansen has written more fiction and non-fiction than poetry, but poetry is still the magical place. A new collection of poems, *Keel and Drift*, was published in 2016 by Landing Press. She teaches on the Whitireia Creative Writing Programme in Wellington.

Benita Kape is a Gisborne poet who has had a strong interest in politics from an early age. Her poems have appeared in OBAN 06 & Fugacity 05, online poetry anthologies at the New Zealand Electronic Poetry Centre; and also in *On The Road to Basra: 2Hweb: A Kasen Renku*, a collaborative work written on the Iraq invasion of 2003.

Koenraad Kuiper's poetry has been published in New Zealand, Canada and the Netherlands. In New Zealand his poems have appeared in *Islands*, *Landfall*, *Poetry New Zealand*, *Sport* and *Takahē*. He has published four books of poetry: *Signs of Life* (1981), *Mikrokosmos* (1990), *Timepieces* (1999) and *Bounty* (CUP, 2008).

Carolyn McCurdie is a Dunedin writer of fiction and poetry. Her first poetry collection, in which 'Beacon fire' appears, was *Bones in the Octagon* (Mākaro Press, 2015). She reads from time to time at the Octagon Poetry Collective's monthly live poetry events in Dunedin.

Melanie McKerchar has had her poetry published in various journals and anthologies. She reads regularly for Lady Poets and Catalyst in Christchurch, and has performed at the Word Christchurch Writers & Readers Festival. She is obsessed with haiku, finding poems in the strangest places and making words work for their meaning.

Frankie McMillan is the author of *The Bag Lady's Picnic and other stories* (Shoal Bay Press) and two poetry collections: *Dressing for the Cannibals* and *There are no Horses in Heaven* (CUP). Her latest book, *My Mother and the Hungarians and other small fictions* (CUP) was published in 2016.

Maria McMillan is originally from Ōtautahi/Christchurch and is based in Kāpiti. She has published two collections of poetry, *The Rope Walk* (Seraph Press, 2013) and *Tree Space* (VUP, 2014), which included 'How they came to privatise the night'. Her poem lifts language directly from water privatisation policies. Maria blogs sporadically at http://mariamcmillan.weebly.com/

Heather Avis McPherson says: 'I'm a seventies women's libber and lesbian poet with other masks and personae. I've presented myself in quiet woman's guise.' Her poem refers to *The First Poets: Lives of the Ancient Greek poets* by Michael Schmidt (Vintage, 2006). Quoted bits of Sappho's poems are composite translations sourced mostly from *If Not, Winter: Fragments of Sappho*, (Anne Carson, Knopf, 2002). Heather McPherson died on 10 January 2017, while this book was in production.

Cilla McQueen is a poet and visual artist. She has published 15 collections of poetry, her latest the poetic memoir *In a Slant Light* (OUP, 2016). Cilla was New Zealand's poet laureate 2009–11. She lives and works in the southern port of Motupohue, Bluff. 'Power riddle' was first published in *Landfall 230*.

Elizabeth McRae has spent most of her working life as an actor, which she says uses skills that are not so very different from those needed for writing. Both depend on a love of words and an economy of expression. Both overwriting and overacting are to be avoided.

kani te manukura: ngāi tūhoe; hunter, gatherer, grower, cook; storyteller. kani leads a life of quiet rebellion in a small seaside town, which is both better and worse than it sounds.

Beverly Martens lives and writes in Dunedin. Her poems have appeared in several anthologies. She is an active member of the Otago-Southland branch of the New Zealand Society of Authors and runs Literary Walking Tours celebrating Dunedin's Unesco City of Literature status. 'Enlightenment' was first published in the 'We' Society Poetry Anthology 2015.

Ria Masae is a Samoan-Kiwi who is currently studying at MIT in South Auckland towards a Bachelor of Creative Arts. Her work has been included in publications such as *Snorkel*, *Ika* and *Landfall*. Ria won the 2015 New Voices: Emerging Poets Competition and the 2016 Cooney Insurance Short Story Competition.

Harvey Molloy's poetry has appeared in many publications in New Zealand and overseas. His most recent book, *Udon by the Remarkables*, featuring 'Dear ET', was published by Mākaro Press as part of the Hoopla series in 2016. Harvey has a Graduate Diploma of Teaching (Secondary) from Victoria University, a PhD from the University of Florida and a MA (with distinction) from Massey University. He lives and teaches in Wellington.

Martha Morseth's poetry has appeared in many New Zealand literary magazines and anthologies as well as in the *New Zealand Listener* and *North & South*. She has published two collections: *Staying Inside the Lines* (Inkweed, 2002) and *Hippopotamus in the Room* (Steele Roberts, 2012).

Janet Newman lives at Koputaroa in Horowhenua. Her poetry, reviews and essays have been published in New Zealand print and online journals. In 2014 she completed a Master's of Creative Writing at Massey University. She is currently a doctoral candidate. Her proposed thesis investigates a tradition of eco-poetry in New Zealand.

James Norcliffe has published nine collections of poetry, most recently *Dark Days at the Oxygen Café* (VUP, 2016). With Harry Ricketts and Siobhan Harvey he edited *Essential New Zealand Poems: Facing the empty page* (Godwit, 2014), and with Joanna Preston the anthology *Leaving the Red Zone: Poems from the Canterbury earthquakes* (Clerestory Press, 2016). 'Underwear' was first published in *Landfall 227*.

Peter Olds was born in Christchurch and has lived in Dunedin since the 1970s. He was a University of Otago Robert Burns Fellow in 1978. Recent publications include *Skew Whiff* with Kathryn Madill (Otakau Press, 2011) and *You Fit the Description: Selected poems* (Cold Hub Press, 2015).

Stephen Oliver is an Australasian poet who lived in Australia for 20 years but is now back in New Zealand. His work has appeared in *Writing to the Wire Anthology*, edited by Dan Disney and Kit Kelen (University of Western Australia, 2016), and he recently published *GONE: Satirical Poems: New & selected* (Greywacke Press, 2016). 'Streets of Kiev' has been published in Serbia, the US, Australia and Russia.

Vincent O'Sullivan is a poet, novelist, short story writer and dramatist who lives in Dunedin. His latest poetry collection is *And So It Is* (VUP, 2016) and his stories *The Families* (VUP) appeared in 2014. Vincent was New Zealand poet laureate 2013–15. 'To miss the point entirely' was first published in *Starling 1* (2015).

Amy Paulussen wrote several novels before she dared attempt poetry. A Paris writers' group inspired her to experiment and taught her the value of creative community. Amy currently chairs the Canterbury branch of the New Zealand Society of Authors, and had a poem published in *Leaving the Redzone: Poems from the Canterbury earthquakes* (Clerestory Press, 2016).

Vivienne Plumb has published 15 books of fiction, poetry and drama, including the non-fiction *Twenty New Zealand Playwrights*. During 2016 she held the University of Auckland/Michael King Centre residency. Her newest publication is a major collection of past-published work, *As Much Gold as an Ass Could Carry* (split/fountain publishing).

Maraea Rakuraku: 'Ko Ngāti Kahungunu ki te Wairoa me Tūhoe ōku iwi.' Playwriting (*The Prospect, Tan-Knee, Te Papakāinga*) and poetry vie ardently for Maraea's heart. She is a graduate of the University of Canterbury and the International Institute of Modern Letters, and founding director of Native Agency Ltd. Her poem 'For those of you who insist ...' first appeared in *Hawai'i Review 79: Call and response* (2014).

Vaughan Rapatahana continues to commute around homes in Aotearoa, the Philippines and Hong Kong. He is widely published internationally across a variety of genres in both his main languages, Māori and English. He won the inaugural Proverse Poetry Prize in 2016.

Richard Reeve is a Warrington poet. His fifth collection, *Generation Kitchen*, was published by Otago University Press in 2015.

Reihana Robinson has been published in the US and New Zealand. She was one of three poets published in *AUP New Poets 3* (AUP, 2008), and her first solo volume, *Aue Rona*, was published by Steele Roberts in 2012.

Paul Schimmel is a psychoanalyst and writer from New Zealand, currently living in Sydney. His psychobiographical study *Sigmund Freud's Discovery of Psychoanalysis: Conquistador and thinker*, was published by Routledge UK in 2014. His first collection of poetry, *Reading the Water* (Steele Roberts, 2016), includes the poem 'Prague 2013'.

Carin Smeaton lives in Newton, Auckland, with her children Kazma and Yuga. She works and, one night a week, studies Te Ara Reo Māori at Te Wānanga o Aotearoa.

The war was always roaring silently through **Marty Smith**'s childhood. Her debut collection *Horse with Hat* (VUP, 2014), which includes 'He couldn't stand the sea', looks at the effects of the gift of silence on servicemen and their families. Although her uncle was awarded the Distinguished Flying Medal, all the kids knew not to ask.

Luke Sole lives within Christchurch's eastern suburbs, a transformative place where all creatures shelter from the virulent machines that strip the earth threadbare. Luke has a BA (Hons) in political science from the University of Canterbury.

Judith Stanley writes stories, poems, reports and manuals. Several of her short stories have been published in anthologies or placed in competition. She is also currently writing a political thriller called 'The Sad Man'. She lives on the Kāpiti Coast.

C.K. Stead's most recent publications are *Book Self: Reviews, replies and reminiscences* (AUP, 2016), and *The Name on the Door is Not Mine* (Allen & Unwin, 2016). He is New Zealand's current poet laureate (2015–17).

Michael Steven was born in 1977. Recent poems have appeared in *IKA*, *broadsheet* and *Contrapasso*. He has recently completed two poetry manuscripts, and is working on a collection of interrelated essays. Michael lives in West Auckland.

Mere Taito, an indigenous Rotuman Islander, moved to New Zealand in 2007. Her work has appeared in *Landfall*, *A Fine Line* and Pacific Island anthologies in Fiji. She is part of the Civil Defence and Emergency Management training team for the Waikato region. Mere writes when time is kind and when the much-loved, fast-talking and video game-loving little human being in her house is asleep.

Zoe Taptikilis studies neuroscience and English at the University of Otago. She is a pedantic over-thinker and, as a Leo, finds her confidence in her own abilities can exceed reality. During Dunedin's winter she is found loitering by the refrigerator in her 'Life-sack'™ (sleeping bag), catching the sweet 4-degree breeze.

Alex Taylor is one of New Zealand's leading young composers, as well as a multi-instrumentalist, poet, critic, lecturer, conductor and impresario. He writes about music for the *Pantograph Punch* and RNZ, and has his own blog: http://thelistenerblog.blogspot.co.nz. Alex is currently writing an opera, 'The Last Delirium of Arthur Rimbaud'.

Nicola Thorstensen was born in Rotorua and now lives in Dunedin. Her poetry has appeared in *Takahē* and the *Otago Daily Times*. She placed first in the published poet section of the Robert Burns Poetry Competition 2016.

Anthonie Tonnon is a songwriter and performer from Dunedin, now based in Auckland. His song 'Water Underground' was a finalist for the APRA Silver Scroll in 2015, and the album it came from, *Successor*, was finalist for the Taite Prize in the same year.

Brian Turner has been publishing poetry and numerous other books—including biographies of All Blacks Colin Meads, Josh Kronfeld and Anton Oliver—since the 1960s. His books include 11 volumes of poetry, for which he has received several notable awards and fellowships. Brian was New Zealand poet laureate 2003–05. At one stage he represented New Zealand at hockey.

Louise Wallace is the author of two poetry collections, *Since June* and *Enough* (VUP). She was the Robert Burns Fellow for 2015 at the University of Otago, and is the founder and editor of *Starling*, an online literary journal for New Zealand writers under 25 years old.

Mercedes Webb-Pullman graduated from the International Institute of Modern Letters at Victoria University of Wellington in 2011. Her poems and prose have appeared in *Turbine*, *4th Floor*, *Swamp*, *Reconfigurations*, *The Electronic Bridge*, *Otoliths*, *Connotations*, *The Red Room*, *Typewriter*, *Cliterature* and *Pure Slush*, among others, and in her books. She lives on the Kāpiti Coast. 'We're all exiles, Kevin said' is in the 2014 'Eat Your Words' contest book *Easy Bites* (Whitireia).

Ian Wedde lives in Auckland and works as a freelance writer and curator. 'The Little Ache: A German notebook' sequence was written in Berlin in 2013–14 during a Creative New Zealand Writer's Residency. His *Selected Poems* is forthcoming from Auckland University Press. Ian was New Zealand poet laureate 2011–13.

Keith Westwater's debut poetry collection, *Tongues of Ash* (Interactive Publications, 2011) received the 2011 IP Picks Best First Book prize. *Felt Intensity* (Submarine) was published in 2015. His work has appeared in *Landfall*, *JAAM*, *Snorkel* and *Idiom 23* and has won or been shortlisted for awards in New Zealand, Australia and Ireland.

Helen Watson White is a Dunedin writer and editor. She has published poems, short stories, photographs and articles, along with theatre, art, opera and book reviews. After 12 years working in Wellington (1973–85) she performed her own mime and political-poetry show, *Living with the Man*, in Germany, Dunedin and Wellington.

Pat White is a poet and painter living in Fairlie. Frontiers Press published his *Fracking & Hawk* (new poetry) in 2015, which included 'Barbarians have crossed the border', and a biography, *The West Coast's Peter Hooper: Notes from the margins*, in 2016. His exhibition *Gallipoli: In search of a family story* shows at Timaru's Aigantighe Gallery in March 2017.

Andrew Paul Wood is an independent researcher and cultural historian, freelance writer and poet. His most recent book, co-authored with Friedrich Voit, is *Karl Wolfskehl: Three worlds* (Cold Hub Press, 2016), a translated selection of the poet's works.

Sue Wootton is a PhD candidate at the University of Otago, researching the affinity between literature and medicine. She co-edits the medical humanities blog Corpus: Conversations about Medicine and Life. Her most recent publications are a novel, *Strip* (Mākaro Press, 2016), and her fourth poetry collection, *The Yield* (OUP, 2017). Sue was a guest at the 2012 Asia Pacific Poetry Festival in Vietnam.

Aroha Yates-Smith is a kaikaranga, a composer and musician/performer, a researcher/writer and a weaver. She was professor and dean of Te Pua Wānanga ki te Ao, School of Māori and Pacific Development, University of Waikato. A Fulbright Scholar and a recipient of the Royal Society of New Zealand Te Rangihīroa Medal, Aroha has had her sung poetry featured in several documentaries, including *Tau Te Mauri Breath of Peace*, and on CDs such as *Mauritau Peace*.

Liang Yujing grew up in China and is a PhD candidate at Victoria University, Wellington. He writes in both English and Chinese, and also translates poetry between the two languages. His work has appeared in *Poetry New Zealand*, *JAAM*, *Takahē* and *Sport*. He is the Chinese translator of *Best New Zealand Poems 2014*. 'The greater wall' appeared in *Wasafiri* (UK), issue 67 (Vol. 26, No. 3).

SWARM OF POETS
AOTEAROA
BORDER CONTROL
TO WRITE A POEM
NZ WINTER APPROACHING
NIGEL
2016

A swarm of poets

Murray Edmond

A high concentration of poets has been discovered in West Auckland. Officials stumbled upon the enclave when attending a champagne supper launch of an Arts Initiative Fundraiser at Te Uru: the poets were observed through the windows of a nearby hall engaged in reading poems to each other. Border Security has been informed and an eradication plan is being formulated. 'We plan to cordon off the whole Titirangi area and anyone entering the cordon will be required to surrender poetry books or similar reading material. No reading material will be allowed to be taken out of the quarantined area,' a spokesperson said. Creative New Zealand says Border Security has their full support. 'We don't know where these poets are coming from, but they are not part of our development plan; nor are swarms of poets included in our mission statement. Frankly, we don't want low-level, hedge-hopping poets writing bad poems about relationships and existential crises and rainbow utopias at a time when Eleanor Catton has just won a prize that has put us on the world stage.' A New Lynn resident said she saw 'a straggly-looking young person of uncertain ethnicity' in the New Lynn Work and Income office yesterday and that they appeared 'to be scribbling lines of uneven length in an old school notebook'. A creative writing tutor at Auckland University said this would not be connected with their programmes because a student nowadays would be likely to be using an iPad or laptop. She went on to say, 'In times of economic recession the number of poems being written tends to rise, so it might just be a seasonal thing, with winter approaching.' Creative New Zealand said they thought this was unlikely. However, the spokesperson added: 'It only takes one person to write a poem and someone else will want to do the same. This is the kind of thing that used to happen all the time, but in the modern Arts Industrial Complex these tendencies have largely been brought under control.' Border Control said that eliminating all poets from the steep gullies of the Titirangi suburban region could prove demanding.